REIKI HEALER

A COMPLETE GUIDE
to the PATH and PRACTICE
of REIKI

Lawrence Ellyard

LOTUS

COVER & PAGE DESIGN/LAYOUT:
Paul Bond, Art & Soul Design

AUTHOR'S PHOTO: Jane Clough

First Edition, 2004
        Printed in th United States of America
        Reiki Healer: A guide to the Path and Practice of reiki
ISBN: 978-0-9409-8564-3
Library of Congress Control Number: 2003111572

Published by:
Lotus Press,
P.O. Box 325
Twin Lakes, Wisconsin 53181
web: www.lotuspress.com
e-mail: lotuspress@lotuspress.com
800-824-6396

CONTENTS

FOREWORD

When I was asked to write the foreword for this book, I was very pleased because I believe Lawrence has a unique approach. I feel he is approaching it from the perspective of someone who has a deep understanding and heart-felt enthusiasm for the subject he writes about. It is apparent from the way he writes that he is a person who is deeply involved in his own spiritual development. He has written an excellent guide to understanding the spiritual practices of Reiki as well as explaining how to use it for healing the mind, body and spirit.

Lawrence has managed to shed new light on the history of Dr. Usui, the founder of Reiki, incorporating many interesting historical facts that have emerged from Japan in recent years. His fascinating account of the origins and subsequent development of Reiki allows the reader to understand how Dr. Usui came to develop this unique system that could adapt and evolve depending on the background and culture of the teacher.

From my work as a psychotherapist, hynotherapist, life coach, joint founder of The Reiki School and co-author of *Reiki: the essential guide to the ancient healing art,* I feel that the perceptions and insights in this book contribute greatly to the practice of Reiki. His understanding of the way in which it works; the vibrational healing that occurs at a causal level and the resulting changes allow the reader to become acquainted with the progression that occurs as a result of its practice.

Lawrence manages to clearly impart an understanding of the processes involved and includes many useful practical applications. In my observations, there is always a spiritual leap after the attunement process has taken place. However, in order to attain the greatest benefit, it is best to continue to use Reiki on a fairly regular basis. While Reiki moves everyone along the spiritual continuum, it is at its most helpful when used frequently. In this book, Lawrence shows how easily Reiki can be incorporated into everyday life for health and healing.

From his particular perspective, Lawrence is able to rise above the dualism of the various Reiki Schools to focus upon the important fundamental principles of Reiki. Enough information is given so that it is possible to gain a full understanding of the available options while supplying details for those wishing to conduct further research.

For we are all individual and there is bound to be considerable variation in the way each teacher imparts similar knowledge to students. If Reiki is taught in the spirit of its founder, it brings about a subtle inner shift that forever changes the perception of those drawn to it, opening hearts and minds to infinite possibilities. Lawrence understands this and appreciates that while every person's perspective and path is unique, it is important they find a teacher of integrity whose lineage can be traced back to Dr. Usui. The book contains plenty of helpful guidance while encouraging readers to use their own intuition to decide how to proceed.

Overall, the book is easy to read and has great insight. It is an excellent overview of both the Eastern and Western systems of Reiki. As well as being thorough, it is thought provoking, informative and enjoyable.

Lawrence writes with the joy of someone to whom Reiki is a passion. He obviously enjoys teaching, writing and practicing this healing art. This book contains many useful techniques to inspire readers to discover how they can use Reiki to transform their lives.

Penny Parkes
Reiki Master
2003

CHAPTER ONE

'Look closely and contemplate deeply.
The people and things that appear around you…
All are in constant flux.
Everything becomes a teacher of impermanence.'

— H.H. THE SEVENTH DALAI LAMA

History of Reiki

Reiki is a Japanese system of hands on healing as well as a spiritual method for personal growth and transformation. The way Reiki is passed from one person to the next is in the form of a lineage tradition. What this means is that a student requires the necessary empowerments from a qualified teacher of the original Reiki tradition. This transmission is given by the teacher in the form of a series of Reiki Attunements. Attunement into Reiki guarantee's the students' ability to achieve a healing outcome and as a result the ability to heal themselves and others is bestowed.

Although the teachings of Reiki are new to the West, (formally introduced to America in the early 1970's), Reiki's origins stretch back to Dr. Mikao Usui who founded the system of Reiki in Japan at the end of the 19th Century. Dr. Usui was primarily a Buddhist although he studied many religious systems of his day. Through Dr. Usui's teaching career, he taught many people his system of Reiki. They in turn passed his system to their own students, yet even today many facts concerning the origins of Reiki and the life of Dr. Usui remain largely unknown.

With the enormous popularity of Reiki today, the system has now been taught to millions of people worldwide. Out of this popularity, the Reiki teachings have developed into many new styles. The majority of these styles have been listed at the end of chapter 1. Since the mid 1970's to the present day, we have seen exponential growth in the area of Reiki. When Mrs. Takata (the first western Reiki Master) brought Reiki to the west, Reiki merged with western culture and with this came much diversity and new developments. Mrs. Takata popularized the notion of Reiki being maintained as an oral tradition, yet in recent years knowledge of Dr. Usui's and Dr. Hayashi's training manuals have come to light. As an oral tradition prevents the use of written manuals, students and teachers had to rely on their memory. As a result, within a few short years, Mrs. Takata's system of Reiki began to change. Added to this were the many teachers who added or removed aspects of the system, making it their own. Inevitably this left the Reiki teachings somewhat altered from their original form.

Fortunately in the early 1990's further discoveries of the original Reiki teachings were found. Dr. Usui's memorial was discovered and many of Reiki's missing links were uncovered. Further revelations included the discovery of a living Reiki tradition in Japan with additional methods as taught by the Reiki Gakkai (Japans Reiki Learning Society.) These discoveries were later made available and for the first time teachers of Reiki gained new information regarding the original system. This information did much to piece some of the lost teachings together with the more established systems of Reiki in the west.

Based on these new discoveries, much of the way Reiki was taught in the past has now changed. Much like an archeological find, these fragments of the past can tell us a great deal about Reiki today and it is from these findings that the following rendering of Dr. Usui's life and path is told.

The Life Story of Dr. Usui

The following is an account of the life and times of Dr. Usui. This information extends to a variety of sources, which can be found in the acknowledgements page at the end of this book.

Mikao Usui was born in the village of Taniai, which is now called Miyama cho, in the Gifu Prefecture on August 15, 1865, where his ancestors had lived for eleven generations. His ancestry dates back to the Chiba clan who were once an influential samurai family in Japan. His family also belonged to the Tendai sect of Buddhism and when he was four, he was sent to a Tendai Monastery to receive his primary education.

Mikao Usui had three brothers'; two of his brothers' names were Sanya, and Kuniji. He also had an older sister called Tsuru. His fathers name was Uzaemon and his mother was from the

Kawai family.

Mikao Usui was born into a class system and therefore received a privileged education. When he was 12 years of age Mikao began martial arts training. He studied two martial arts called 'Aiki Jutsu' and 'Yagyu Ryu' and attained a high level of proficiency in weaponry and grappling. He spoke many languages and became well-versed in medicine, theology and philosophy. Usui's memorial states that from his youth he had surpassed his fellow students and that he was well versed in history, medicine, Buddhist and Christian scriptures, and Waka poetry. It also states on Usui's memorial that Usui was versed in divination, incantation, and physiognomy and like many intellectuals of his day was also fascinated with the 'new science' coming from the West.

DR. MIKAO USUI

During this time the Meiji Emperor had begun a new regime. Under this new regime, the 'old ideas' were discarded in favor of modernization and the country was opened to westerners for the first time. During this time a strong desire for transforming the modes of daily life into occidental fashions arose, which were identified with civilization. In every department of social and political life, men furnished with some knowledge of modern science were promoted to high positions. Men of 'new knowledge' were almost idolized and the ambition of every young man was to read the 'horizontal writings' of occidental books. The nation as a whole asked eagerly for the benefits of the new civilization. The motto of the era was 'Enlightenment and Civilization'.

Usui's father, Uzaemon, was an avid follower of the new regime and adopted progressive political views. Usui had great respect for his father and was very influenced by this national obsession to become 'westernized.'

In 1922, Usui reportedly founded the Reiki society, called Usui Reiki Ryoho Gakkai, and acted as its first president. This society was open to those who had studied Usui's Reiki. This society still exists today and there have been six presidents since Usui:

Mr. Juzaburo Ushida 1865-1935,

Mr. Kanichi Taketomi 1878-1960,

Mr. Yoshiharu Watanabe (unknown - 1960),

Mr. Hoichi Wanami 1883-1975,

Ms. Kimiko Koyama 1906-1999, and the current president Mr. Masayoshi Kondo

On September 1, 1923 the devastating Kanto earthquake struck Tokyo and surrounding areas. Most of the central part of Tokyo was leveled and totally destroyed by fire. Over 140,000 people were killed. In one instance, 40,000 people were incinerated when a fire tornado swept across the open area where they had sought safety. These fires were started when the quake hit at midday, when countless hibachi charcoal grills were ready to cook lunch. The wood houses quickly ignited as they collapsed from the tremors. Three million homes were destroyed leaving countless homeless. Over 50,000 people suffered serious injuries. The public water and sewage systems were destroyed and it took years for rebuilding to take place.

In response to this catastrophe, Usui and his students offered Reiki to countless victims. His clinic soon became too small to handle the throng of patients; therefore, in February of 1924, he built a new clinic in Nakano, outside Tokyo. His fame spread quickly all over Japan and he began receiving invitations from all over the country to come and teach his healing methods. Usui was awarded a Kun San To from the Emperor, which is a very high award (much like an honorary doctorate,) given to those who have done honorable work.

Usui quickly became very busy as requests for teachings of Reiki continued to grow. He traveled throughout Japan (not an easy undertaking in those days) to teach and give Reiki empowerments. This started to take its toll on his health and he began experiencing mini-strokes from stress. Usui then left for a teaching tour in the Western part of Japan. Finally, on March 9, 1926, while in Fukuyama, Usui died of a fatal stroke. He was 62 years old.

Usui's body was cremated and his ashes were placed in a temple in Tokyo. Shortly after his death, students from the Reiki society in Tokyo erected a memorial stone at Saihoji Temple in the Toyatama district in Tokyo. According to the inscription on his memorial stone, Usui taught Reiki to over 2,000 people. Many of these students began their own clinics and founded Reiki schools and societies. By the 1940s there were about 40 Reiki schools spread all over Japan. Most of these schools taught the method of Reiki that Usui had developed.

With the advent of Mrs. Takata's introduction of Reiki to America in the 1970's, Reiki has flourished in the west and, ironically, much of the Reiki that one finds in Japan today is actually imported from western teachers.

In 1999, some of the original methods as taught by the Reiki Gakkai were revealed for the first time in Vancouver, Canada. These practices were taught by Mr. Doi, a member of the Reiki Gakkai and many teachers now use these methods, dating their origin back to the teachings of Mikao Usui.

The Reiki Gakkai

The Usui Reiki Ryoho Gakkai, or the Usui Reiki Healing Method Learning Society, was the first society formed in honor of Usui Sensei. Some speculation still surrounds whether Dr. Usui actually began the society as he is listed as the first chairperson in 1922. However, it is more likely that this was done more so as an honorary title out of respect for the legacy which Dr. Usui had left his students.

Research suggests that the second chairperson, Jusaburo Ushida (1865-1935,) began the learning society shortly after Usui Sensei's passing in 1926. Ushida was also the author of the Usui Memorial, Dr. Usui's grave memorial at Saihoji temple in the Toyotama district of Tokyo.

During the Second World War, the Reiki Gakkai went underground, moving its headquarters so as not to be detected as being a part of the Japanese peace movement. After the Second World War, the Reiki Gakkai re-grouped and continued its practices formally. Today the Reiki Gakkai continues its practices and teachings based on Dr. Usui's inspiration.

In Reiki Gakkai many techniques are taught to enhance a students ability to generate spiritual growth, how to heal oneself and others, and to increase awareness of subtle energy. The formal instruction of Reiki in the learning society takes place in a very methodical and progressive manner. The emphasis is on complete accomplishment of each practice before proceeding to a new level. The Gakkai therefore has ranks and levels within their system.

Ranks are based on the student's ability to channel the energy and their adeptness or proficiency in performing the techniques.

Shoden (the first level) is comprised of three stages, the Sixth, Fifth and Fourth. A student will go from proficiency rank 6 ('the beginning level' or First Degree) where the student learns hand-on healing methods and other techniques from the beginners level. One then progresses once they have proven to have accomplished the methods taught at each stage.

In Japan a student might take as long as 10 years to attain the 3rd proficiency rank (Okuden.) At this level, the student is taught more advanced healing methods.

Below are the Ranks taught in the Reiki Ryoho Gakkai.

Proficiency Rank 6 - Shoden Level ('beginning teachings')

Proficiency Rank 5

Proficiency Rank 4

Proficiency Rank 3 - Okuden Zenki, Okuden Koeki and Shinpiden Levels

Proficiency Rank 2

Proficiency Rank 1

There are 4 levels taught in the Gakkai, Shoden ('beginning teachings'), Okuden Zenki ('highest or secret level', first term or Second Degree), Okuden Koeki ('highest or secret level', latter term or Personal Mastery) and Shinpiden ('Secret method' teacher training or Sensei.)

At each level, additional methods are given. The practice of Reiki is seen as a method or path to reach higher levels of Spiritual consciousness with healing being a 'by-product' that occurs from connecting to the 'True-self.' When a student has mastered Okuden Koeki and the collective Usui Reiki Ryoho Gakkai Shinpiden teachers feel the student is ready, they may vote for the student to receive Shinpiden (teacher training.)

Currently there are only 6 Shinpiden level teachers in the whole Reiki Gakkai. Precisely how a student is chosen to receive training or when Shinpiden is actually taught is not presently known.

The Reiki Gakkai is also a closed Reiki Society. They do not encourage contact with foreigners and all members are asked not to discuss the details of their training with those who are not members. The Reiki Gakkai currently consists of 500 members and is based in Tokyo. Students learn on a weekly basis in the society. During these meetings, students Chant the Reiki Principles, recite

Waka poetry* and practice Hatsurei-ho (energy enhancing practices.) Each week, Shinpiden (teacher) Sensei's give students regular Reiju (energy empowerments.) These regular empowerments
act to purify and opens the students' energy channels.

*Waka poetry is a traditional Japanese poetic form with fixed
line lengths of 5-7-5-7-7 syllables. Much like Haiku poems, Waka
poetry expresses spiritual aspirations, which aid in the expression
of the Enlightened Mind.

As mentioned previously, some of these methods have now
come to the west, via Hiroshi Doi Sensei. Today, other variations of
this Reiki movement exist under other names, these include:
Gendai Reiki (Modern Reiki Healing Method), Usui Reiki Ryoho
and Japanese Reiki Method.

Reiki's Chronology

AD

1865 Usui is born on August 15th in the first year of the
Keio period.

1879 Chujiro Hayashi is born.

1900 Mrs. Takata is born.

CA 1902-03 Usui opens his first Reiki Clinic in his home
near Osaka.

1921 Usui opens second Reiki clinic in Harajuku, Tokyo.

1922 Usui founds the Reiki society: 'Usui Reiki Ryoho
Gakkai'.

1923 Earthquake devastates Tokyo.

1924 Usui establishes new clinic outside Tokyo
in Nakano.

1925 Chujiro Hayashi begins studying with Usui.

1925 Usui passes his teachings to his foremost students.

1926 Usui dies of a fatal stroke on March 9, aged 62.

1926 Students of the Usui Reiki Ryoho Gakkai erect a
memorial stone for Usui at Saihoji temple in the
Toyotama district of Tokyo.

1930s Hayashi establishes a clinic in Tokyo.

1936 Hayashi brings Reiki from Japan to the West when
he visits Hawaii.

1936 Mrs. Takata learns Reiki from Hayashi.

1938   Mrs. Takata receives the complete empowerments
        for teaching Reiki.
1940   Chujiro Hayashi dies on May 10th.
1970s   Mrs. Takata begins teaching Reiki in the United
        States of America and over a ten-year period,
        initiates 22 students to teacher level.
1979   Mrs. Takata dies (Western Universal Reiki begins
        to be disseminated through the world).
1993   Dr. Usui's memorial is found and many of his
        original teachings are revealed.
1999   The methods of the Reiki Gakkai are revealed and
        Western teachers begin to learn and utilize these
        methods for the first time.

Hayashi Reiki

For some teachers of Reiki, Hayashi Reiki is a term to describe the
methods taught by Chuijro Hayashi that are different in methodology to the style of Dr. Usui.

Hayashi was a student of Dr. Usui for a period of 10 months in
1925. Notably, Hayashi is considered by many teachers of the Reiki
Alliance to be the only successor of Dr. Usui; however, new research has revealed that Usui taught several teachers.

To place this style in greater perspective, the following is an
overview of the life of Hayashi Sensei and his style of Reiki, which
emerged as a result of his teachings.

Chuijro Hayashi was born in 1879. Some time in 1925 Chuijro
Hayashi met Dr. Usui for the first time. Prior to this meeting,
Chuijro was a naval commander in the imperial navy where he
also gained training in Western Allopathic and Eastern Chinese
Medicine.

In June of 1925, Hayashi received his teacher's training in Dr.
Usui's system. Some sources say that Chuijro Hayashi was also
Methodist Christian*. {*Hayashi's religious background was confirmed by Mrs Yamaguchi. Mrs. Yamaguchi was a student of
Hayashi and she confirmed that he was a Christian of the Methodist church. She recently passed away.} Other sources indicate that
he was a Soto Zen practitioner who utilized the practices of Shinto.
For all we know, he may have been both as Japan was a melting pot
of numerous religions and spiritual ideals.

On March 9th, 1926, Dr. Usui died. Counter to the story promul-
gated by Mrs. Takata, Dr. Hayashi was not considered, nor chosen,
as Dr. Usui's direct and only successor. Shortly after Dr. Usui's

passing the Reiki Gakkai was formed and Hayashi was said to be involved with this learning society.

Late in 1931 Hayashi was also said to have left the society. Hayashi continued to work at Dr. Usui's Reiki clinic, which was called the Usui Memorial Clinic. Hayashi later renamed the clinic, 'Hayashi Reiki Kenkyu kai' or the Hayashi Reiki Research Society. During this time, Hayashi made several changes to Dr. Usui's system. Hayashi continued to teach his style of Reiki and began

CHUJIRO HAYASHI

teaching students the third degree in his system, or Shinpiden level. Before his death on May 10th, 1940 he had attuned 13 students to the teacher level, including Mrs. Takata in 1938. Some of his noted students include:

• Chie Hayashi, Chujiro's wife, who continued running his clinic and later became the second President of the Hayashi Reiki Kenkyu kai'.

• Chiyoko Yamaguchi, who studied with Hayashi in 1938. Until her recent passing, Mrs. Yamaguchi taught her own branch of Reiki called 'Jikiden Reiki' in Kyoto, Japan.

• Tatsumi, who trained with Hayashi in 1927 to become a teacher. Tatsumi learned a series of hand positions that were formulated to cover specific acupuncture points and subsequent areas of energy flow over the body.

As a result of Hayashi's changes, Usui's system of Reiki had changed significantly. Consequently, Mrs. Takata inherited Hayashi's system under the Usui name and thus propagated Hayashi's teachings as the Usui System of Natural Healing. Prior to the advent of the discovery of the Japanese Reiki society, most western students had thought that the system of Reiki which was passed to Mrs. Takata was the only existing style of Reiki. Interestingly, the title 'The Usui System of Natural Healing' or 'Usui Shiki Ryoho', used by Reiki teachers in the west actually indicates the system of Reiki attributed to Mrs. Takata and Chujiro Hayashi.

Takata Reiki

Mrs. Takata's Reiki style is perhaps the most well-known and wide spread system of Reiki in the world today. Being a student of Hayashi, Mrs. Takata brought her adapted system of Reiki to America in the beginning of the 1970's and during a 10 year period taught 22 western students to the teacher level of her system.

The 22 teachers taught by Takata include: Dorothy Baba, Ursula Baylow, Ric'< Bockner, Patricia Bowling Ewing, Barbara Brown, Fran Brown, Phyllis Furumoto, Beth Gray, John Gray, Iris Ishikuro, Harry Kuboi, Ethel Lombardi, Barbara McCullough, Mary McFadyen, Paul Mitchell, Shinobu Saito, Bethel Phaigh, Virginia Samdahl, Wanja Twan, Barbara Weber Ray, Kay Yamashita and George Araki.

Many of these students went on to prolifically teach Reiki, notably, Phyllis Furumoto (The Reiki Alliance) and Barbara Weber Ray (The Radiance Technique,) as well as many others. As a result of these teachers and the others that followed, Reiki spread globally within a few short years. Today there are literally millions of Reiki Practitioners world-wide and their teachings are largely based on what was passed on from Mrs. Takata. As we will see in the following pages, further changes to the Reiki system occurred after Mrs. Takata's death, contributing to the many Reiki styles that have emerged in subsequent years. It is important to note here that while Mrs. Takata's Reiki system is a complete system in its own right, which brings excellent results, its methodology and practices differ considerably from Hayashi's and Usui's Reiki styles.

The following is a brief account of the life of Mrs. Takata.

Hawayo Kawamura* (*her maiden name,) was born on December 25th 1900 in Hanamaula, Kauai, Hawaii. In 1917 she married her husband, Saichi Takata. They had two daughters, one named Alice Takata-Furumoto, who later had a daughter named Phyllis Furumoto (*The Reiki Alliance*).

Following the death of her husband in 1930 and then her sister in 1935, Hawayo Takata decided to go to Japan to visit her parents. During these years she worked many long hours to cover her grief and to provide for her family and as a result her health began to suffer.

While in Japan she began treatment for her health problems and it was subsequently determined that she would require an operation. Just before her operation she heard the voice of her dead husband inicating that the operation was not necessary and that there was another way. This prompted her to speak with her doctor of alternative treatments and he referred her to Hayashi's Reiki Clinic.

Hawayo Takata received daily treatments at this clinic for a period of four months. During this time her symptoms completely abated.

Hawayo Takata then took Reiki training (Shoden) with Hayashi on December 10th, 1935. She trained with Hayashi

HAWAYO TAKATA

for a little over one year. In 1937, Mrs. Takata received the second level in Hayashi's system (Okuden). Shortly after this, she returned to Hawaii. A few weeks later, Hayashi visited Mrs. Takata with his daughter and stayed until February 1938. During this time, Hayashi Sensei officially made Mrs. Takata a Reiki teacher and bestowed the Shinpiden or Teacher level upon her.

On May 1940, Chujiro Hayashi died. Mrs. Takata was Hayashi's 13th attuned teacher of Reiki and it is understood that Hayashi taught over 14 students to the teacher level. It is important to note that both Dr. Usui and Dr. Hayashi both issued Reiki manuals and allowed their students to take notes to record their classes for the sake of posterity. This differs from the modern view held by many western Reiki teachers of the Takata tradition that Reiki was an oral tradition.

Between 1940 and 1970 Mrs. Takata ran several Reiki clinics and taught many classes in Hawaii. She later retired from teaching until the early 1970's when she began teaching Reiki in the United States. In 1976 she trained her first four students to the teacher level, including: Virginia Samdahl, John Gray, Ethel Lombardi, and Barbara McCullough.

In December of 1979, Mrs. Takata made her transition. She had trained 22 teachers in what she termed 'The Usui System of Natural Healing' or 'Usui Shiki Ryoho'. At this time Takata's teachers were of the understanding that Mrs. Takata was the only living successor of the Reiki tradition and that all of Usui's and Hayashi's students and teachers had either died prior to or during the Second World War.

It was also understood by these teachers that what Mrs. Takata had taught them was exactly the same in methodology as the teachings of Hayashi and Usui. In 1975 Mrs. Takata even advertised that she was the only teacher of the Usui System of Reiki in the world today. Until this time, knowledge of a Japanese style or other separate lineages of Reiki was largely unknown to Western Reiki practitioners.

With the discovery of the Japanese Reiki styles, Mrs. Takata's system of Reiki has since been discovered to be significantly different than her predecessors, however much gratitude and acknowledgement is recognized. The merit shared as a result of Mrs. Takata's actions has had far reaching benefits to humanity and as a direct result of her teachings Reiki has become a world wide phenomenon.

Here is one, (for there are many), of the traditional Western versions of Takata's story and how Reiki came into being. One should note that many aspects of this story have now in fact been determined as being incorrect and these will be noted at the end of this recitation.

Dr. Mikao Usui, a Christian minister in the late 19th Century, discovered Reiki. Dr. Usui was the Principal at Doshisha University, a small Christian University in Kyoto, Japan. One day he was speaking to his students of how great teachers, like Jesus, healed the sick. One of his students challenged him to show them living proof of these healing miracles reported in the Bible, and asked whether Dr. Usui had any ability to perform such feats of spiritual power. Dr. Usui, being an honorable man, confessed that he had no personal experience and that he could not teach his students these methods. He subsequently resigned his position to dedicate his life to rediscovering how Jesus healed. Usui believed that he would be able to study the best theology in a Christian country, so he traveled to America to study at the University of Chicago. Despite receiving a medical doctorate and studying theology, he still had not found what he was looking for.

Usui returned to Japan, determined to find his answers. He began visiting Buddhist monasteries, speaking with priests and scholars, but to no avail. Finally, he encountered an Abbot at a Zen monastery who allowed him to study the secret writings of the Buddhist Sutras. It was within the Sutras that he found the formulas and symbols for healing, yet this was still not enough as he had no ability to activate this healing ability in himself. The kind Abbot advised him to meditate on the sacred mountain in the hope of receiving a vision. Usui trusted the Abbot and followed his advice. Usui made the pilgrimage to Mt. Kurama to fast and meditate for a period of 21 days. This he did, setting 21 stones in front of him to count the days. At dawn of each morning, he threw one stone away to mark the completion of each day. During this time he grew very weary from the lack of sleep and food, yet he remained vigilant in the hope of receiving his vision. It was not until the 21st day that he received the answers to his questions. Upon throwing the last stone that lay before him, he saw in the distance a strong beam of light traveling towards him at great speed. He grew very fearful at this display of spiritual power, yet he knew it must be the answer he was looking for. He remained very still and waited. This great light came and struck Usui in the forehead, overwhelming him until he soon lost consciousness. His spirit left his body and he was shown beautiful rainbow colored bubbles of light, each containing the symbols he had seen in the Sutras. The lights entered his body and he was shown the mantras, the symbols and attunements for activating healing in others. Usui heard a voice say, "Do not forget this, these are the keys to healing, do not allow them to be lost." Some time later, he regained consciousness.

Usui was surprised to find that he no longer felt fatigued or tired. On the contrary, he felt euphoric and energized. Finally, after many years of searching, he had found the keys to healing power. He hurried down the mountain with great enthusiasm, looking forward to telling the Abbot of his experience. In his haste he tripped and fell, badly cutting his foot on a sharp rock nearby. Blood immediately began to flow from the wound. Usui placed his hands on the wound and great warmth flowed from his palms. Within minutes the bleeding had stopped, the pain had ceased and the wound had completely healed.

When Usui reached the bottom of the mountain he stopped at a food stall, as he had a considerable appetite from his fasting. Upon receiving his food he noticed the young girl serving him had been crying, and her face was red and swollen on one side. The girl told him between sobs that she had a very bad toothache, but her father could not afford dental treatment. Remembering how quickly his foot had healed, Usui offered to place his hands on her face. Again,

great warmth flowed from his hands and in a few minutes the pain
ceased and the swelling subsided. Usui then ate his huge meal
with no trouble, considering his long fast. Later that day, Usui returned to the monastery and found the Abbot in bed suffering from
a bad attack of arthritis. Usui held the old man's hands while he
spoke of his experiences on the mountain, and within a short time
all the pain from the arthritis had gone.

On the advice of the Abbot, Usui decided to work amongst
Japan's poorest and most suffering. He returned to Kyoto and
worked with the beggars in the slums. He worked there for several
years, helping the sick and destitute. Although he had helped some
of these people, many were returning to the streets in much the
same condition as he had found them. Usui grew very disap-
pointed and asked them why they had returned to a beggar's life.
Their response was always the same, it was too much responsibility to work at a job and have a family. Returning to begging
seemed an easier way of life.

Usui soon realized that it was not enough to heal a person's
physical condition; spiritual healing was vital in total transformation. Having ignored the beggars spiritual needs he had denied
them the appreciation for life and how to live in a new way. They
had received this healing art freely and were not required to give
anything in return; thus they simply did not appreciate the gift that
was given. Usui then decided to leave the beggars and began
teaching people who truly wanted to be healed. He developed five
spiritual principles to assist his students in developing themselves
in their healing:

• Just for today, do not anger
• Just for today, do not worry
• Honor your parents, teachers and elders
• Earn your living honestly
• Show gratitude to every living thing

As Usui traveled from town to town, he would carry a flaming
torch during the day as a symbol of the light and spiritual teachings that he was offering. It became his calling card and his popularity soon spread. He acquired many disciples who would travel
with him and assist him in his teachings. One of his principle students was Dr. Chujiro Hayashi. Usui continued teaching Reiki for
the remainder of his life. Before his death Usui passed all his
knowledge to his senior student Dr. Chujiro Hayashi so that Reiki
could be passed on to others and not lost, as it had been in the past.

Usui appointed Hayashi as the Grand Master of the Reiki lineage and Hayashi carried forth the work of his master in a similar manner.

New Revelations

The story just described is based on Mrs. Takata's oral tradition. Most Reiki teachers simply accepted Mrs. Takata's story as being factual until some practitioners began to research the origins of Reiki.

In her original Reiki story, Mikao Usui is depicted as a Christian, teaching theology at the Doshisha Christian University in Japan. However, derived from research, he was in fact a devout Buddhist. Further, Usui never taught at Doshisha University and was never a Principal of any school. Official letters from Doshisha have been obtained, stating no knowledge or record of Mikao Usui. Research has also determined that Dr. Usui was in fact a Buddhist and was very skeptical of the Christian doctrine.

In Mrs. Takata's story, Dr. Usui is also said to have traveled to the United States to receive his Doctorate in Medicine from the University of Chicago in the late 1880s, yet no records of Usui's name exist at the University of Chicago. Other variations of the western story say that he was never a doctor and instead studied theology in the United States.

Indeed, if Dr. Usui had in fact traveled to the United States and had studied medicine in the 1880s, the Medical Faculty of Chicago University had not yet been established. It wasn't until the 1890s that the Medical Faculty began in the city of Chicago. This was some ten years after Usui was meant to have studied there.

Many variations of the western Reiki story also describe Dr. Usui's experience on Mt. Kurama. Some of these stories describe many sensational events and although Usui gained revelations, his experience did not extend to the realization of supreme enlightenment, nor experiences which parallel in grandeur that of Jesus Christ in the Bible.

Like all great stories, they tend to become more elorbarate as time goes by. Even today, there are still many teachers who continue to teach and write the old Takata story, despite the now-documented historical facts.

We will now go on to examine some of the more traditional Takata Reiki styles that emerged soon after Mrs. Takata's death in 1979. These systems formalized and gave solid structure to Reiki and ultimately dominated the way Reiki would be taught to millions of people throughout the world.

The Reiki Alliance

In 1982, the first formal Reiki Masters meeting was called in Hawaii in honor of Mrs. Takata. By this time, the name for a teacher of Reiki had been replaced with the name 'Master' of Reiki. Formerly, the title for 'teacher' in Japan was referred to as Sensei. At this 'Masters' gathering, many of Mrs. Takata's students were present. When they began to share with one another and compared information, they found that from one student to the next, there were many variations in methodology, attunements and even the Reiki symbols. It appears that Mrs. Takata taught her students in many different ways.

Recognizing a need to form standards and guidelines, the teachers present began to form a structure that everyone could agree upon. These decisions would have a great impact on how Reiki would be taught in the future and these influences still impact the international Reiki community to this day.

Prior to this meeting in Hawaii, the role of who would be chosen as Mrs. Takata's successor or as it is often described 'the Grand master' or 'Lineage bearer,' was yet to be officially determined. Note: the Term 'Grand Master' was never used in Japan by Dr. Usui. The Reiki Gakkai used instead proficiency levels to determine a teacher's ability.

Two likely candidates out of the 22 teachers taught from Mrs. Takata emerged. The first being: Dr. Barbara Weber Ray, one of the last students to learn with Mrs. Takata. (1978-1980,) and Phyllis Lei Furomoto, Mrs. Takata's grand daughter, who had received an extended yet informal apprenticeship with Takata, on and off for many years*.

{*Phyllis Furumoto received Reiki attunements from her grandmother over many years, though formal instruction was not given to her until 1979. She received the First degree attunement as a small child, Second degree at 27 years of age, and the Third degree at 30 years of age. (1979).}

Regarding the role of Successor, two opinions presided and still exist to this day. These were that Mrs. Takata asked Dr. Barbara Weber Ray to continue her tradition (see The Radiance Technique next heading) the other being Phyllis Lei Furumoto.

It was also said that Mrs. Takata wished both Barbara Weber Ray and Phyllis Furumoto to be successors of her Reiki system. Some months later, Mrs. Takata died and the issue of who was the lineage bearer became a somewhat divided and clouded issue.

During this period, a division arose between these teachers as to who would recognize and support Phyllis Lei Furumoto's claim to the role of successor and those who would recognize Barbara

Weber Ray's claim as Takata's successor. Other teachers opted for an independent stance

Phyllis Lei Furumoto decided to follow in her grandmothers' footsteps and during that meeting in 1982, she was elected to this position by the majority of Reiki Masters present. Other Masters supported Barbara Weber Ray's claim to successor and followed her direction.

In 1983, a second meeting was formed by the Reiki Masters who recognized Phyllis as Grand Master and the Reiki Alliance was born. The Reiki Alliance formulated and adopted this statement at this meeting:

"We are an alliance of Reiki Masters. We regard all Masters as equal in the oneness of Reiki. We acknowledge Phyllis Lei Furumoto as a Grand Master in the direct spiritual lineage of Mikao Usui, Chujiro Hayashi, and Hawayo Takata. The purpose of the Alliance is to support us as teachers in the Usui System of Natural Healing."

The Reiki Alliance, in a similar fashion to the Radiance technique, attempted to standardize the practice of Reiki. Until 1988, Phyllis Lei Furumoto was the only teacher within the Alliance who was recognized to initiate Reiki Masters. As the pressures of requests grew in this position, Phyllis then announced that any suitably experienced Reiki Master could initiate their students. This announcement in many ways opened the 'Flood Gates' and a torrent of new Reiki Masters emerged within a few short years.

To compensate for the huge increase in demand on Phyllis, she joined forces with Paul Mitchell, another of Mrs. Takata's trained teachers, and they formed the "Office of Grand Master" in 1992. Since this time both Phyllis and Paul have worked tirelessly to encourage the international Reiki community to come into alignment with their understanding and views of the Usui System of Natural Healing. Much to their credit, their actions have been an invaluable service to the International Reiki Community and to the direction of traditional Reiki Training within their system.

A brief overview of the Reiki Alliance System

As set forth by the Reiki Alliance, their Reiki system has four aspects, which are healing practice, spiritual discipline, personal growth and the mystic order. The Alliance also has a guideline of which elements should be presented when teaching Reiki.

These guidelines are called the Nine Elements of Reiki.

These consist of the following: The form of classes, Reiki treatment, Spiritual Lineage, Spiritual precepts, Initiations or

Attunements, Reiki History, Money, Oral Tradition and the
Reiki Symbols.

These Elements are outlined as follows:

The form of Classes: Here the Alliance outlines that there are
three degrees, including the mastery level. That within each
level, a certain content must be taught and that there is a minimum time span between classes.

Reiki Treatment: Specific hand positions for treating oneself
and others.

Spiritual Lineage: Acknowledging the lineage of Usui,
Hayashi, Takata and Furumoto.

Spiritual Precepts: The five Reiki principles,
• Just for today, do not anger
• Just for today, do not worry
• Honor your parents, teachers and elders
• Earn your living honestly
• Show gratitude to every living thing.

Initiations: The specific energy alignments given to students by
the initiating Master. The result is a connection and ability to
transfer Reiki healing energy. Four attunements at the First Degree, one at the Second Degree and one at the Third Degree.

Reiki History: The telling of the Reiki History in connection
with how Dr. Usui discovered Reiki as part of the oral tradition.

Money: The fees recommended by Mrs. Takata for learning
each Reiki level: Prices in U.S. Dollars. $150 for Reiki I, $500 for
Reiki II, and $10,000 for Reiki Master (Level III).

Oral Tradition: Each level should be taught by the teacher in an
oral fashion, with little or no notes given.

Reiki Symbols: The Reiki symbols act as specific ways of directing and opening Universal Healing Energy. There are four
in total. Three are given at Reiki II and one given at Reiki III.

The hand positions were based on Mrs. Takata's instruction. Recent research determined that these hand positions were created
by Mrs. Takata and not by Dr. Hayashi as previously thought.

The Reiki Alliance today is a strong network of Practitioners
and Masters worldwide. Through the efforts of Phyllis Furumoto
and Paul Mitchell this 'westernized' form of Reiki, called Usui
Shiki Ryoho and sometimes referred to as The Usui System of
Natural Healing has continued to be a source of connection, stabil-
ity and interaction for people who use Reiki from many styles and

lineages. Still today, many Reiki practitioners and Masters align themselves with the Reiki Alliance and consider this form to be the final word on Reiki and its practice throughout the world.

The Radiance Technique

The Radiance Technique is a particular style of Reiki that states itself to be the Authentic Reiki as taught by Mrs. Takata to Dr. Barbara Weber Ray. Barbara Weber Ray claims that Mrs. Takata gave her more keys to the Mastery level than any of her previous students. This system is comprised of 7 degrees that offer additional Reiki symbols and methods.

Barbara Weber Ray received her Reiki Initiation, or Third degree training, with Mrs. Takata in 1979. In the same year she opened the Reiki Center in Atlanta, Georgia and began documenting Reiki healings at the center.

In 1980 Barbara Weber Ray established the American International Reiki Association. Today the Association is called The Radiance Technique International Association Inc. (TRTIA). It was said by Barbara Weber Ray that Mrs. Takata announced her to be her successor at the inaugural ARA meeting in Atlanta in 1980. Other sources say that Mrs. Takata did not attend this meeting.

Barbara Weber Ray was also responsible for writing the very first Western book on Reiki, titled *The Reiki Factor*, first printed in January 1983. It was not until later revised editions that the Registered Trademarks of The Radiance Technique, Authentic Reiki, and Real Reiki were established.

It seems from the material presented in subsequent editions of the Radiance factor and material posted on the TRTIA website that unless you have learned Reiki through the Radiance Technique, you have learned an incorrect form of Reiki. The TRTIA website also states that only those authorized instructors of the TRTIA have the Real Reiki system. It is clear that the Radiance Technique are determined to protect the authenticity of their system and consider their system to be the original and pure form of Reiki.

Claims that Barbara Weber Ray obtained additional secret teachings from Mrs. Takata remain a point of contention with little likelihood of resolution.

Although the Radiance Technique as an organization has their particular and unique view on Reiki, their methods are excellent and generate a tremendous benefit to the practitioner who uses them.

Establishing high standards of practice and authorization of Teachers is an admirable stance and surely needed in this age

where many people within the "new age" movement are looking
for titles, instant spirituality and the mystical experience without
doing the necessary practice.

Other Reiki Styles

Beyond these two major Reiki styles, which first emerged shortly
after Mrs. Takata's passing, there are today numerous Reiki styles.
Each style has its own methods and practices, which are far too
many in number to individually comment upon in this book. But to
give you some idea of just how many styles presently exist in the
world today, here are but a few.

1. Adama Starfire Reiki
2. Alef Reiki
3. Amanohuna Reiki
4. Angelic Raykey
5. Angel Touch Reiki
6. Anugraha Reiki
7. Ascension Reiki
8. Authentic Reiki
9. Blue Star Reiki
10. Brahma Satya Reiki
11. Buddho Ennersense Reiki
12. Dragon Reiki
13. Dorje Reiki
14. Fusion Reiki
15. Gakkai Reiki
16. Gendai Reiki
17. Golden Age Reiki
18. Ichi Sekai Reiki
19. Imara Reiki
20. Innersun Reiki
21. Japanese Reiki
22. Jikiden Reiki
23. Jinlap Maitre Reiki
24. Johrei Reiki
25. Kava Reiki
26. Karuna Ki
27. Karuna Reiki
28. Ken Reiki-do
29. Kundalini Reiki

30. Lightarian Reiki
31. Magnussa Phoenix Reiki
32. Mari El
33. Medicine Buddha Reiki
34. Medicine Dharma Reiki (Men Chhos Reiki)
35. Medicine Reiki
36. Monastic Seven Degree Reiki
37. New Life Reiki
38. Ni Kawa Reiki
39. Osho Neo Reiki
40. Radiance Technique
41. Rainbow Reiki
42. Raku Reiki
43. Reiki Jin Kei Do
44. Reiki Plus
45. Rei Ki Tummo
46. Sacred Path Reiki
47. Sai Baba Reiki
48. Saku Reiki
49. Sangle Mendela Reiki Do
50. Satya Japanese Reiki
51. Shakyamuni Reiki
52. Siddhearta Reiki
53. Silverwolf Reiki
54. Seichim or Seichem
55. Sun Li Chung Reiki
56. Tanaki Reiki
57. Tera-Mai and Tera-Mai Seichim
58. Tibetan Soul Star Reiki
59. Tibetan Reiki
60. Universal Reiki Dharma
61. Usui-Do
62. Usui Reiki Ryoho
63. Usui Shiki Ryoho
64. Usui Teate Reiki
65. Usui/Tibetan Reiki
66. Usui Universal Healing Reiki
67. Vajra Reiki
68. Violet Flame Reiki

69. Wei Chi Tibetan Reiki

These are but a few and no doubt in time many new styles will either emerge, be discovered or invented. Whether this is for legitimate reasons of lineage, methodology, or simply as a means of marketing Reiki in a new way, one thing is evident and that is that Reiki will continue to evolve in the future.

If you have an interest in any of these styles, the Internet is an excellent source where you can research the benefits of each system and perhaps you may even find a teacher in your area.

We acknowledge that some material has been derived from the following sources:

Reiki Dharma, the Virtual Home of Frank Arjava Petter: www.reikidharma.com

Reiki Fire by Frank Arjava Petter. Lotus Press. ©1997
Reiki: The Legacy of Dr. Usui by Frank Arjava Petter. Lotus Press. ©1998

The Original Reiki Handbook of Dr. Mikao Usui by Dr. Mikao Usui and Frank Arjava Petter. Lotus Press. ©1998

The Spirit of Reiki by Walter Lübeck, Frank Arjava Petter and William Lee Rand. Lotus Press. ©2000

Modern Reiki Method of Healing by Hiroshi Doi. Fraser Journal Publishing. ©2000

CHAPTER TWO

*'The seeker who has confidence in the way will
go beyond the way and find the end of suffering.
The seeker who goes beyond the way enlightens the world,
just as the moon shines as it passes from behind the clouds.'*

— THE DHAMMAPADA

What is Reiki?

Reiki is a Japanese method of hands on healing. Through the use of certain techniques the practitioner administers healing energy via the hands to another.

Reiki energy is the healing energy of the Universe. Reiki is a life force matrix of non-dualistic energy, which permeates all things. A Reiki practitioner harnesses this power via the Reiki attunements, which, in effect, switch on a person's ability to transfer Reiki healing to oneself and others.

These attunements are a transmission of energy, which activate the ability to utilize Reiki. Attunement into Reiki is given by a Reiki teacher. A Reiki teacher is someone who has the precise methods for transferring this ability to others. Once this alignment is complete, the practitioner can utilize this healing energy in a variety of ways to restore the body, mind and emotions into a harmonious state.

Reiki is applied via the hands and is activated by touch. The practitioner of Reiki places their hands on the corresponding chakras, meridians and organs, transferring healing energy. When Reiki is applied to another, both the practitioner and the recipient receive the healing energy.

Often people assume the healing energy of Reiki when applied to another comes from the practitioners own life force energy, where in fact, the Reiki energy simply passes through the practitioner, much like electricity through a wire.

With regular use, ones Reiki ability increases and the healing effects spread out into ones life more and more. Reiki increases vitality. When we consider that energy is the foundation of all life, it makes sense that if we have more energy constantly available to us, the natural by-product of this is a gradual enhancement of our health and personal well-being. By the transference of Reiki healing, there is a noticeable increase in the body's natural vitality and therefore a greater ability for the body to heal itself.

Divine Intelligence

Reiki is an intelligent energy. Many people liken the energy to the source of all-pervading power. Many traditions have a variety of names for this power, for example: God, Buddha, Mind, Nature, Universe, Great Spirit, The Force, etc. Regardless of what label we place on the energy, the importance lies in the notion that a higher force does permeate all existence and once we become attuned to the Reiki system, there is effectively a merging of the divinity within our own spirit with that of the Universal energy.

Once this alignment is made, our connection to this source of power is ignited. We then have a greater capacity to use this healing power, by introducing Reiki into situations to heal and awaken ourselves and others.

When we utilize Reiki energy we are channeling a healing energy that has intelligence. What this means is that the Reiki energy will direct itself to the areas of imbalance as well as the cause. When Reiki is applied either to oneself or another, which is as simple as placing ones hands-on, healing energy is transferred to activate whatever is most required, either in yourself, or the person being treated.

Who is the Healer?

When we are facilitating healing for another, it is important to know that we are simply conduits for the healing energy. In effect, we are not the ones performing the healing activity, we are the instruments. One could draw the analogy of ourselves as an empty vessel and the Reiki energy as pure water. Once we have had our own life energy matrix attuned to the Reiki energy, it is like our vessel is filled. Once the vessel becomes too full, the water overflows. So when we are giving another Reiki, the healing energy enters through the top of our head and transfers out our hands to the person receiving. A practitioner does not expend any of their own vital energy. In fact, their own life force is strongly enhanced through the experience. The reason for this is whatever healing energy is transferred to the other, must first flow through the practitioner.

When we give Reiki, we are in effect working in a partnership with the energy. Reiki attunement creates a union between ones own life force energy and the energy of the Universe. As the practitioner, we are the ones responsible for the healing application, where as the Reiki energy is the healing force moving through ourselves to benefit others.

Reasons to Learn Reiki

Reiki is one of the simplest yet profound healing systems known to human kind. The following are some of the many reasons for learning Reiki.

- Reiki not only heals the physical body, it works towards healing the cause of illness, thereby eliminating the effects of the imbalance.
- The benefits last a lifetime. Once you have the attunements, regardless of whether you use the energy consciously or not, it is always with you.
- Reiki can be successfully combined with other healing methods and is a useful tool to have, which can be incorporated into daily life.
- Reiki does not conflict with religious beliefs, therefore it is a teaching that can be used by anyone.
- Reiki is a self-empowering healing method. Reiki gives you an ability to heal yourself and to generate greater self-reliance. It is also an alternative, natural healing method, which is an additional way to heal the body when you are ill or out of balance.
- Reiki promotes from within the qualities of love and compassion. With ongoing use a deep peace begins to permeate your life, anger subsides and better, more intelligent and trusting, relationships endure.
- Reiki is an intelligent energy, which goes to greatest need. Reiki not only heals the symptom of illness, it also heals the cause.
- Reiki begins to flow when you touch something and it is always on. Think of all the things you touch each day, then think of how Reiki could be of benefit.
- Reiki does not interfere with medical treatments; it actually enhances medications, and assists the body to healing at optimum speed.
- Reiki is an excellent tool for healing problems and for manifest-

ing positive outcomes to numerous situations.

• Reiki can be used on animals, plants, children or any living being.

• Reiki calms nervous tension, calms fears and subdues negative
emotions; it is also a useful technique for being guided and protected throughout life.

• Reiki is the highest form of healing energy. Reiki is always safe
and can never cause harm.

• Belief in Reiki is not a requirement for it to work. Reiki is not a
belief system, nor is it a placebo effect. Even if you do not have
faith in Reiki, healing effects still result.

• Reiki is available 24 hours a day, right there in your hands. It
never runs out.

CHAPTER THREE

*'You must love all and help all
because it is only in that you can help yourself'.*

- SRI RAMANA MAHARSHI

The Attunements

The foundation for becoming a practitioner of Reiki is the attunement process. The attunements 'tune you in'. So it is necessary to have them as they create the union between the Reiki energy and your own energy.

The process of initiation into Reiki is an exact science, or if you like, a formula. This is why it is essential if one wishes to gain a complete and pure connection to Reiki energy, one needs the correct empowerments from a qualified Reiki teacher.

Attunement into Reiki is a physical and energetic transmission from the teacher to the student. It is not enough to simply read a book on Reiki, practice some techniques and as a result have the ability to facilitate Reiki healing. We need the empowerments from someone who knows how.

So how do the Attunements work? The initiations are an ancient formula. The keys to these formulas lie in the Reiki symbols. The attunements are a combination of these formulas as well as the teachers' lineage and ability.

The teacher then transfers these formulas during the attunement procedure to the student. These energetic formulas merge with the students energy system and this creates an alignment and pathway to Universal Energy.

There are a number of factors that support an effective Reiki alignment. These are as follows:

1. The initiating teacher should have an unbroken lineage in the Reiki system. This means the initiating teacher must have received the empowerment to the third degree, (the level that em-

powers the individual to teach and initiate the Reiki levels.)

2. The initiating teacher must have been empowered from a qualified and empowered Reiki teacher, (one who has the ability to
teach and empower teachers).

3. At the minimum level, the initiating teacher is required to facilitate four separate attunements for first degree Reiki to create a
permanent and lasting result.*

   * Reiki styles vary in the number of attunements given at each level.

If these factors are met, and provided the initiating teacher has the
correct procedures and carries these out appropriately, then the
full alignment to the Reiki energy will occur every time. This is
always the case, regardless of belief or intention on behalf of the
recipient. Many people think Reiki has something to do with a talent or some special God given gift, yet this is not the case. For if it
was, it would not work for everyone. The reality is for an individual to have these alignments one only needs an energy system
to qualify. The initiation procedure works beyond concept, intention or belief.

   It is also important to note that one does not need to add new
things to the Reiki system. The system is complete in itself. Just as
one would not give a patient medicine they do not require, so a
teacher of Reiki does not need to add additional elements to the
system or attunement procedures.

   The following are some additional points to consider:

• Attunements work specifically on a persons Chakra system.
  Reiki creates a new pathway of energy, which is distributed
  throughout the entire body.

• The attunement process utilizes the pathway of the central channel. The result of initiation has a direct effect on the whole of
  ones being, including the physical, emotional, mental, psychic
  centers and spiritual centers.

• Although Reiki attunements utilize a persons energy system they
  also operate independently of that system. What this means is
  our Ego, emotions or feelings cannot disrupt the flow of vital energy. One can also perform self-healing when one is ill, emotionally upset or even distressed, these feelings have no effect upon
  the transmission of Reiki energy.

Naturally, when healing others, it is common sense to be first in
balance, however even if this is not the case, Reiki still works and
will actually assist in the transformation of these situations. The
healing energy comes through the facilitator first, so both the facili-

tator and the receiver heal at the same time. The very act of facilitating Reiki can assist in elevating one's mood, increasing relaxation and enhancing wellbeing whenever the hands are placed upon oneself or another.

- The Reiki energy does not stop when we fall asleep, regardless of our state of consciousness the energy transmits when the hands are in contact with the body. Practitioners can actually do a lot of personal healing while asleep. By placing the hands on the body when comfortable in bed, this practice not only promotes restful sleep, but assists in the subtle healing of the body.

- Once a student has received the four attunements for First Degree Reiki, this alignment can never be lost or taken away; it remains a permanent alignment for the rest of the person's life.

- Reiki is activated by touch, so as long as the hands are in contact with the body, the energy begins to flow, transmitting healing energy to whatever is required in any given situation.

- As a general guide, Reiki energy will also activate when the hands are not in contact with the body. The energy can also activate in a variety of ways, such as: while doing meditation, Tai Chi or Chi Kung, relaxing or simply enjoying a creative task. Although Reiki works well above the body it is essentially a hands on modality, so it is preferable to proceed in your sessions with both hands on.*

Unless the area is too painful to touch or if the area is a private part of the body, such as the breasts or genitals.

The correct formula

The importance of having the correct initiation procedures can be likened to a chemical formula. For example, the Reiki Attunement process is like the formula H_2O, which translates as water. Now if we change this formula slightly to H_2O_2, in chemistry we have hydrogen peroxide.

This was only a slight change with a dramatic effect. Similarly, if we change the attunement procedures and introduce new symbols and/or new procedures outside the Reiki system, we cannot be certain of the outcome. This is why it is essential to have the correct alignment in the traditional system and to perform these procedures correctly every time. In this way we support the system that works and can be sure that the results have a lasting effect.

There are many systems of Reiki today, and many initiation sequences that have been published both in books and over the

Internet. These sequences are not intended for anyone to experiment with. As mentioned previously, one needs the correct attunements and training to be most effective in their transmission. Without this, one could liken it to performing surgery without any expertise or training. The danger of proceeding without the necessary understanding and guidance from someone who knows how, is a hit and miss affair. It is one thing to tinker with sacred teachings on oneself, but it is quite another to tamper with another's path.

Even if one has access to the Reiki symbols and the attunement procedures, yet one has not been attuned to the teachers level from a qualified Reiki teacher, there is no fuel to drive the system. Therefore one cannot create a positive alignment for another. Effectively the power switch is on but the electricity is switched off at the main.

It is also important to note here that there are many variations of the attunement procedures. Some vary greatly from traditional initiations, and others vary only slightly in procedure and content.

Depending upon the person facilitating the attunements and the procedures used, outcomes vary. Just because one attunement procedure differs from another does not mean it will not work. The majority of the time, a healing ability is transferred; however, the degree of potency and effectiveness as well as the quality and feeling of these procedures differs greatly from one system to another. Certainly procedure, lineage and the ability of the teacher play an integral part in the transference of an effective healing ability.

What initiation brings
Purification.

Purifications occur throughout the Reiki System and roughly translate as the clearing of past blockages, toxins, and dysfunctional patterns within our being.

To mention but a few, purifications can be felt as various aches and pains, headaches, nausea, dizzy spells, loose or regular bowel movements, and even feeling ungrounded. These experiences are only often felt during a Reiki seminar and sometimes for a few days before and after the attunements.

It is also important to note that one does not usually experience all of these symptoms and sometimes one will not experience any at all. On the other hand, if one is experiencing purification, it is comforting to know that these symptoms are a direct result of the Reiki initiations and are generally a temporary experience.

A good way to think of it is that you are leaving behind some old habitual tendencies that you no longer need.

Sometimes people may experience emotional release in the form of mood swings, feeling emotional or the experience of old or present emotional concerns. Some people have fits of laughter or get the 'Reiki Giggles'. Some people simply feel touched, or blessed, while others experience lots of joy or may be afflicted by a very serious condition called 'smiling'.

The thing to remember is that if you are not experiencing these purifications of the body and mind, don't worry. It does not mean Reiki is not working, it just depends on how the energy is working through you.

One should view purifications as a good thing. If you have all kinds of mental agitation, negative emotions, or physical discomfort then you have the opportunity to release the things you no longer need. Surely this is a good thing. If on the other hand you experience a lot of joy, bliss and happiness then this is also good. The thing to remember is: IT'S ALL GOOD!

When we receive the connection to Reiki, we are effectively coming back to who we truly are, and many people feel this. Many report a feeling of 'coming home', or that the experience of giving Reiki has a familiarity.

Part of this continued alignment often translates to a greater sensitivity to the needs of our body and mind. Many people report that the need for various crutches like tobacco, coffee and alcohol is definitely changed in them as a result of the attunements. With regular practice, many people also note a much lower tolerance for the substances that create imbalances in the body and mind. With further practice one becomes more attuned to what ones body needs as well as the kinds of people and environments one wishes to be with.

With time and application, the practice of Reiki creates a pathway to our inner knowing, and this means knowing what is best for us on all levels of our being.

C H A P T E R   F O U R

'It is wise to know yourself,
before instructing others in self-knowing.
Thus you defeat sorrow.'

— THE DHAMMAPADA

How to Prepare for First Degree

Once you make the commitment to attending a Reiki class with your chosen teacher, it can be experienced that certain forces begin to come into being. Quite often people experience subtle changes or shifts within and around themselves leading up to Reiki initiation. The Reiki energy begins to merge with your energy field and begins to raise your vibratory level. Many people report that they can feel subtle sensations in their hands and body even before turning up to the workshop. This is the Divine Intelligence of the Reiki energy working with you, removing obstacles to your healing and preparing your body and mind for the transmissions to come. In a way, the deeper part of yourself, your unconscious mind is preparing for the attunements.

Reiki First Degree

Reiki I is the first level in the traditional Western Reiki System. The first degree or beginner's level offers many benefits, and of all the levels offers the most noticeable energetic connection. This is because it is the first time the initiate receives the Reiki Alignment with the Universal energy. The experience of making this connection is noticeable in many ways. Some common experiences include: physical energy sensations, such as warmth, heat, tingling, waves of energy and so on, as well as many subtle sensations around the head, hands, spine and upper body.

Traditionally in Reiki I there are four initiations. These initiations gradually open the individual to the full capacity of the level one energy. These four separate attunements highlight specific areas of the body*.

NOTE: The following information is based on the Takata attunement model and variations may differ from one Reiki style to the next.

Results of the Four Attunements

Attunement 1

- Creates a temporary alignment with the Universal energy.
- Highlights the Crown and Heart Chakra and the connection between the two.
- Highlights the palm Chakras.
- Both inner and outer energy merge and this pathway is extended through the hand Chakras.

Attunement 2

- This initiation works on the heart/thymus and palm Chakras.
- Widens the recipient's channel to Universal energy and expands upon the qualities of the first attunement.

Attunement 3

- This initiation, although being the same as the second, deepens the connection in the heart/thymus and palm Chakras and further expands the channel within the individual.
- It too enhances and expands the benefits of the second initiation.

Attunement 4

- The final initiation works specifically on the pituitary and pineal glands and seals the recipient with the first degree Reiki permanently.
- At completion of the fourth initiation the individual has a complete alignment with the Universal energy and this can never be lost or hindered.
- This initiation completes the previous three initiations and aligns the recipient permanently to Reiki.

Pre-attunement Guidelines

As a general guide, it is suggested to prepare oneself before receiving attunement to Reiki. This not only supports the attunement process but also mentally prepares oneself for the positive changes the Reiki attunements bring.

The following are some useful guidelines that you may wish to follow.

- Avoid taking any substances that may cloud the mind such as caffeine, heavy foods, cigarettes, alcohol or recreational drugs. These substances have a direct effect on the energy system and generally hinder the flow of higher resonance energy.
- Keep the days preceding and the evenings between the workshop quiet and passive where possible. Often, before and within the class environment, each participant goes into a deep and nurturing space. Therefore, it is best to support this by keeping a peaceful space outside the workshop setting. This assists in maintaining the thread of the daily Reiki experience.
- Remember to nurture yourself. Set time aside to simply be. It is good to do something that gives you pleasure, a walk in nature or even a candle-lit bath. Utilize this time to reflect on your life and think about how you might integrate what you have learned in the workshop. A Reiki workshop is a unique time for reflection and change.

Purification and the Attunements

As mentioned previously in Chapter 3, purifications can occur as a direct result of the Reiki attunements. Occasionally, once having received the attunements, an individual may experience a cleansing and detoxifying process. This process is usually most heightened during the workshop and for the following three days.

Some of the purification that may occur are:

- A short cold or flu just after the workshop.
- Headaches or a mild nausea.
- Fatigue or heightened energy.
- Hot flashes, dizziness, regular yawning or sweating.
- Types of emotional releases such as crying or laughter.
- Various aches or pains due to the release of blockages both energetic and physical.

If you do experience any of these purifications, realize that these are not lasting effects and that they will pass. The degree of how we experience clearing will vary from person to person. This is largely dependent upon our own personal path, or accumulated past Karma, and how much work we have done on ourselves in this life. Generally speaking, if we have led unhealthy lives, and have many unresolved issues, such as holding wrong views and have consciously harmed others in the past, then the degree of this purification will be heightened.

As we move through this process, it is highly recommended to

practice regular self-healing treatments. While giving yourself
Reiki, your hands on sessions will enhance this healing process,
and will support you in your personal growth.

It is usually recommended that new students make the commitment to giving themselves a regular self-healing treatment each
morning and evening for a three-week period after a Reiki workshop. This regular commitment will not only instill a positive pattern within your mind, it will also assist in the full integration of
the Reiki attunements and the energy of the First Degree.

The Way of Self-Healing

'If you don't take care of your body, where will you live?'

— UNKNOWN

Of the many things Reiki can offer, self-healing is perhaps the most
important aspect of Reiki. Each time we apply Reiki to ourselves
we are furthering the pathway to our health and healing. When we
look at it, this is not such a difficult task, as all we need do is remind ourselves to place our hands on our body throughout the
course of a day. Reiki is a natural thing to do. We see this so often.
What do we do when we hit ourselves on the thumb with a ham-
mer (besides hopping around and making a lot of noise)? We hold
it.

With a Mother caring for a sick or upset child, it is her hands
providing the healing touch, by holding and comforting the child.

Touch communicates more in five seconds than five minutes of
talking. Touch is a great healer, so it makes sense that if we hold
ourselves with full alignment to the Reiki energy, we will naturally
be transmitting, not only self-healing but self-love. Reiki is a great
way to become reacquainted with ourselves, to touch and nurture
ourselves.

In the words of Mrs. Takata: *"A little Reiki is better than none at
all"*; so whether we give ourselves Reiki for five minutes or one
hour, there is always some benefit. The approach with Reiki is
much like homeopathy; it is better to do a little on a regular basis
rather than a lot, once a month. A mini session can simply comprise
five minutes on yourself before you get out of bed in the morning,
or by placing your hands on your belly after a meal to aid digestion.

If we hold the view of Reiki as a chore, for example: *"Oh, I have
to do my practice today"*, then we simply have the wrong view. Reiki
should be a joyful and natural thing to do. The important thing to

remind ourselves is that our hands have an additional role to play. These are not just hands that can do amazing things, but are instruments of creating healing, pleasure and balance for others and ourselves.

In addition to your regular Reiki mini sessions, you may also wish to give yourself a full treatment once a day or a few times weekly. This process is the same as giving a full treatment to another. The only difference being that we correspond the hand positions to our self in a way that is comfortable.

If you are feeling stressed, lie down or sit back and place your hands over your eyes or on the back of your head. Reiki is a very simple concept, if something hurts, then reach for your hands before you reach for an aspirin.

It is also important to consider going directly to the area of concern. Don't wait for a headache to become a migraine before you use Reiki. The sooner 'hands on' healing is activated, the sooner Reiki can work its magic. This goes for treating others as well. If a person has a specific complaint one should focus the majority of the time treating the area of concern. In this way you will be giving the person exactly what they need. For example, if someone has an upset stomach they will generally desire direct treatment in this area. If they have to wait 30 minutes until you reach this area in the hands on sequence, they will be thinking to themselves, *"I wish they would treat my stomach"*. This is why it is important to talk with the person to determine what areas are in need of direct application. In this way you go to the symptom that is most in need and invariably this will treat the cause as well.

Naturally with any healing, whether it is self-healing or healing others, we need to use Reiki with common sense. If a situation calls for medical advice and treatment, we should always follow this. Reiki is a complementary adjunct to western medicine, so with this in mind, we should use the best of both worlds.

How We Heal Others

A common concern for practitioners is how much Reiki to give in any given situation. The length of a treatment and the time between sessions is largely dependant on the individual concerned, and the time available for both the practitioner and recipient. Generally, a session can last anywhere from thirty minutes to one and a half hours. The length of time between a session can be anywhere from one day to one week. If a person has a major illness or would like to work intensively on an issue, then it is suggested that four treatments are given over four consecutive days. The results of these sessions are then assessed. In some cases, one may not see the breakthrough of a problem until the third or fourth day. The reasons for this vary; however, each progressive session builds on the previous one, thereby enhancing the effectiveness of the Reiki healing.

Committing to a number of sessions is sometimes too much for a new client, and as a practitioner, it is important to explain the healing process in terms of the ongoing benefits. However, one should not recommend on-going sessions as a way to solicit on-going fees. This motivation is highly unethical, especially if the person no longer needs treatment.

If such a commitment is made, then one should supplement this commitment by a reduced rate for on-going consultations.

Experiences While Giving Reiki

Whether you are conducting Reiki for yourself or another, there are a variety of experiences that can be perceived.

The most common of these experiences are:

1. A feeling of heat or warmth in the hands.
2. Tingling or pulsing up or down the arms and within the body.
3. Cold or cool energy running through the hands.
4. The cessation of mental chatter, and increased calm.
5. Deep relaxation.
6. Visual impressions, seeing colors, lights or images.
7. Hands feeling drawn to an area.
8. Hands feeling repelled from an area.
9. Hands feeling like they are stuck or glued in an area.
10. Hands feeling like they are a few inches inside the area that is being worked on.
11. An occasional sharp or dull pain in your hands or arms.
12. A slight vibration in the hands or arms.
13. An increased desire to yawn.

All of the above phenomena are natural by-products of working with the Reiki energy and experiences vary from person to person. The important thing to remember is that these experiences are a result of engaging with Universal energy and, therefore, it is not essential to interpret, or get 'too precious' about these kinds of experiences. They were not there before and will not be there later, so why get too attached?

As a practitioner gains greater experience, these sensations can become signals or forms of diagnosis to determine what is required concerning the persons healing. However, these kinds of methods do take time to perfect and to accurately interpret what each of these sensations mean for the individual concerned. Unfortunately, it is not all black and white; as each sensation, symptom or experience can have countless meanings, interpretations and causes. So it is best not to leap to conclusions regarding an individual's needs until you become proficient in these advanced methods of healing.

It is also important to note that unless one is licensed to do so, one does not prescribe or diagnose a client's condition.

Cause & Effect and Metaphysics

Our physical mind loves to have experiences and part of this often translates as attachment to phenomena that arises from Reiki. There is nothing wrong in identifying with these experiences, such as perceiving various colors or sensations during a Reiki treatment as this is a confirmation that something is actually happening. One readily observes with a group of new students that when group members share experiences, a natural comparison occurs. Some will have experiences on a visual level, while others will have experiences on a feeling level. The potential blind spot with identifying with these sensations and experiences is prescribing a particular meaning to the sensation. For example, heat meaning repressed anger or emotional pain or seeing the color green to suggest this represents envy. The danger in such generalizations lies in the practitioner placing their interpretation on the person receiving the healing. This response may not necessarily have relevance or meaning for the person concerned. As practitioners of Reiki, one should offer advice that is fairly neutral, so as not to influence the client's view. If a practitioner puts on the Therapists hat after a session and begins to psychoanalyze the client, the process of healing becomes a complicated situation and much confusion can arise as a direct result.

Metaphysical causations for physical sensations are incredibly general, and more often than not bear little meaning to the cause of a person's symptoms. This is not to say that metaphysics have no place in healing. The point is that some practitioners can use these views as a general form of diagnosis, and if not qualified to give diagnosis, can influence a client regarding their actual condition. It is for this reason that cause and effect illustrations are not recommended. Hypothetically, when such metaphysical rules are put in place, a practitioner may simply say: *'Oh, you have a sore lower back, that's because you have repressed anger towards your father'*. Whereas the real reason may be that the client injured their back in a motor vehicle accident some months previously. Such a response can leave the client dis-empowered and may result in the practitioner looking for the wrong approach in healing the client's complaint.

The use of metaphysics has its place in healing, but a word of warning: don't allow these concepts to cloud your judgment. Each healing situation is unique and we need to approach our healing sessions with a clear view, free of concepts.

Responses to Reiki

The ways in which a person responds to a Reiki session are many and varied. A common experience is that a session will take the recipient into a deeply relaxing space. It is also common that they may even fall asleep. For others, Reiki can bring emotional issues to the surface. If a person does need to cry, gently nurture them and keep applying the energy. It does not mean that you have done something wrong if a person is crying, it is the result of Reiki working on the emotions as a form of release. Tears are a way to purify blockages and emotional pain, as well as a way to detoxify the physical body.

If a person has a large emotional release, be caring but stable and ask them to breathe through it. You may even breathe with them. Breathing is one of the most effective ways to move through emotional issues and one should never encourage a client to have an intense experience. For example; expressing pain or anger while screaming out loud. Reiki is a long way from primal scream therapy and much can be released without all the theatrics and drama.

As a practitioner you can offer a shoulder to cry on and an ear to listen. If a client does not wish to share their feelings, that's OK. If we are not trained in counseling or basic psychology, sometimes it is better not to put on the therapist's hat. Be there for the person, be real and be caring, as this is often all a person needs to feel safe and accepted with their emotions.

At the end of a Reiki treatment, give the person time to bring their awareness back and ask them how they are feeling. Often a client will ask the inevitable question: *"So what did you pick up?"* Be careful, it is not your role to let your ego feel important, nor to stand upon a pedestal and impress them with your uncanny psychic abilities. Remember to be humble and never allow your pride to take hold. You are supposed to be there for the client. You are not there for your own self-inflation. After a treatment you may suggest the areas where you felt the Reiki energy drawing, but do not take the step of telling them why or what this means. If someone asks, just tell them that this was probably an area of imbalance and the Reiki energy was assisting in restoring balance to this area of concern.

Acting in this manner will never draw complications to yourself. This will also assist you in generating a more balanced and compassionate view to healing. Reiki is about service and one of the fastest ways to further our path is through the compassionate activity of healing and serving others.

Hands-on Healing Treatmemts

Traditionally, Reiki follows a sequence for applying the hands upon another person. This is in order to cover the major areas of energy flow, as well as energizing the major organs and energy centers of the body. This systematic approach works on the premise of twelve positions on the front of the body and twelve positions on the back of the body. (Schools vary in this approach.)

The hand positions are a way to facilitate a general healing, and to boost the life force and vitality of the recipient. The hands are usually left in these positions for anywhere from three to five minutes, with the whole session taking approximately one to one and a half hours.

Hands-on Healing Procedure

The following are some basic guidelines to facilitate a healing at the Reiki First Degree level.

1. Gather information from the recipient regarding their needs.

Ask: *Have you had a Reiki Session before?* If not, briefly explain the process.*

Here one will state that Reiki is the transference of Universal Healing Energy and that you will be placing your hands on the areas of imbalance to restore the vital energy within their being.

Ask: *Is there anywhere you require healing?*

Once you have a general idea of what they require, ask them to close their eyes and relax. It is usually recommended that both you and the client keep the talking to a bare minimum. This is so they can receive the maximum benefit and so you can concentrate on what you are doing. It is important to check whether they are comfortable and to ask whether your hands are too light or too heavy. One should never introduce movement with hands on healing and the hands should always rest gently on the persons' body.

2. Centering Procedure: Place your hands on your upper chest and close your eyes.

Focus your intent for a brief moment. Imagine yourself being a vessel for the Universal energy and that you are being completely filled from your feet to the top of your head with healing energies. This can be imagined as a white light pouring from the Universal source above the top of your head.

3. Once you feel that the Reiki energy has completely merged with your body, establish the strong wish to benefit the person seated or laying before you. One can even offer a simple prayer making this wish.

This establishes your personal boundaries throughout the healing procedure and prepares you for the actual treatment.

4. In your own way commence the session, following the step-by-step approach of applying Reiki to the body. You can imagine that as you are applying the Reiki energy that this energy is flowing from the source above your head and flowing effortlessly through your body and out of your hands. Imagine this energy is filling the area where your hands are in contact, restoring and healing the area completely. You may even enhance this experience with your breath. On the in breath, imagine the Reiki energy flowing into your body and with the out breath, imagine this healing energy is gently transferring to the person. One should also be mindful not to focus too much on the breathing, and certainly not breathing loudly or in such a way as one might blow out a candle. It is an effortless, graceful and gentle process, in the way that you place your hands and in every aspect of your being.

5. Once you feel the healing is complete, wash your hands and imagine that there is a blue energy field much like a bubble in your mouth. Blow this through your hands and sense that any lower energy is dispelled instantaneously. This disconnects you from the recipient's energy field.

6. Gently bring the person around and share your experiences.

Be sure not to interpret or diagnose their condition, we simply share what we sensed in the session.

Guidelines for Reiki Treatments

- Be sure to remove any pets from the room, your client may be allergic to cats or dogs and animals have a tendency to disrupt a session.

- If you are going to burn aromatherapy oils or incense make sure the person does not have allergies to them. If you are unsure, don't use them.

- Be sure to wash your hands before and in between clients. Neat personal dress and hygiene are essential.

- Give your client the opportunity to ask questions.

- Make sure they are comfortable in their position and always check to see they are comfortable. Some people will keep quiet and suffer silently, just to be polite.

- Make sure the placement of your hands on their body is without undue pressure. Ask if your touch is at a comfortable pressure, especially if your hands are on the face of the person.

- Try and keep contact with their body (hands on) at all times, or within 2 to 3 inches of the body between hand positions. This ensures they know where you are and can relax. NEVER place your hands on or near any area that is private on the body, in particular the breasts and genital area.

- Wear comfortable clean clothing, preferably in layers in case you get too hot. Be sure that your presentation is neat and tidy, that you are well groomed and your personal hygiene is above reproach. This includes being mindful of your body odor, particularly your armpits and feet.

- If you have more than two or three clients per day, be sure to change your clothes between sessions or shower when possible as a means of maintaining your energetic clarity. Be sure also to change the sheets on your table and pillow covers between clients.

- Make sure your breath is fresh and don't breathe on your client's face. This can be very disruptive to the clients comfort. Avoid eating things like garlic or other strong smelling herbs before a session.

- Be sure not to place your hands too close to the client's nose, ears or throat unless there is a specific reason. These areas can be uncomfortable for the recipient, especially if your hands are too heavy.

- Use tranquil music or see if your client has a particular preference of music.

How to Find a Reiki Teacher
and What to Look For

Finding an appropriate teacher is often an intuitive and synchronistic experience. Keep in mind that you may have to wait for the right teacher, so don't let convenience and money be your only deciding factors. It can really be a mistake to look for the cheapest Reiki class offered. Generally speaking, if you pay peanuts for Reiki you get Monkeys. So be careful!

When you are investing in your spiritual life and personal well-being, it makes sense to research your subject to find the right Reiki style for you as well as the right teacher. These days the Internet can be a great source for this kind of information. Embarking upon the healing path can be really exciting and people tend to embrace everything with enthusiasm. Unfortunately, without knowing what to look for, they often throw out ideas like common sense and discernment. These things are very important, so check in with yourself to see if 'all sits well' within your being.

Even within the New Age movement, you may find teachers who are not coming from an altruistic motivation. It can be all too easy to be lead astray by tricksters and deceptive characters who want nothing more than to be a guru, driven by ego and financial gain at your expense. This may seem somewhat harsh, but no matter what the profession, be it a used car sales person or your spiritual Guru, you need to have sound judgment and a discriminating mind, lest you be lead astray.

So here are a few points to look for in a teacher of Reiki:

1. Check the teacher's Reiki lineage. He or she should be able to tell you who they learned from and their Reiki lineage dating back to the founding teacher, Mikao Usui.

    Some Reiki lineages are many teachers long and may be watered down significantly by wrong views and insufficient training. Some people will call themselves a Reiki Master, and may have only been doing Reiki for a few weeks! The term 'Reiki Master' is no guarantee that you will encounter a Master of Reiki.

2. Ask how long they have been teaching and how long their own teacher training was.

    Do they teach regularly and do they use Reiki on themselves and others, in other words do they practice what they preach?

3. Check to see if the training you will receive is of a sufficient time frame. (Approximately 14 hours for a Reiki First Degree work-

shop and 12 hours for a Reiki Second Degree workshop.) Ask how many hours are devoted to hands on healing and experiential Reiki work.

4. You may wish to ask what specific things you will cover throughout the workshop and what you will be empowered to do after the training in each level.

(Refer to Reiki content in Chapter 6 for a comparison.)

5. Check to see if there is any ongoing support after the training, or opportunity to practice with others after the workshop. Will the teacher be available for you after the workshop?

6. Will you receive a Certificate of Reiki upon completion? Is this Certificate recognized?

7. Is the cost reasonable and are you supplied with a reference manual? Will you get what you paid for?

Ask if you are able to take notes in the class or tape-record the information presented.

9. Check in with your intuitive or gut feeling. Does this person sound authentic, and are they coming from the right motivation? Do you resonate well with this person?

10. Can the teacher send you supporting material on the workshop content and the courses available or do they have a website you can visit for information?

11. Make sure your prospective teacher recommends integration time between Reiki levels. Be wary of teachers offering combined Reiki levels or skipping levels that you have not yet completed.

12. Who will be giving the initiations at the seminar and how many initiations will you receive? (Traditional Reiki states: Four at Reiki I and one at Reiki II.)

13. Check to see if any symbols are taught in the Reiki levels and which ones are being taught. There should not be any symbols taught at the Reiki I level, and only three Reiki symbols taught in Reiki II.

14. Does the teacher have the experience to teach you? How long have they been teaching Reiki?

15. How many people does the teacher have in a single class?

16. What form do the classes take? Are they over one, two, three days or are these classes spread out over a number of days or weeks?

17. Where will the seminar be held and is this location practical for
you?

These are some of the main questions you should ask when making
inquiries. As a general guide, be wary of teachers making outra-
geous or extraordinary claims. If you are still unclear, see if the
teacher is prepared to meet you personally to discuss in further
detail and to find out exactly what will be covered throughout the
workshop.

It makes sense to know who you are becoming involved with,
so exercise some caution when finding a teacher. There are so
many Reiki's available these days, and not all teachers are coming
from the right motivation, methodology, understanding or integrity.

Overall, it all boils down to trusting your intuition. The person
should be a living example of the things they practice. Literally,
they should: 'walk their talk!'

Watch your personal expectations – most integrated teachers do
not dress in white robes or act in a 'holier than thou' fashion. A
good Reiki teacher is usually down to earth, realistic and normal in
appearance. Be wary of sensational and over-the-top characters,
especially if they are making big promises and charge even bigger
fees than their promises!

It may take time to find a good teacher and learning Reiki is not
something to rush into.

Make an informed choice, and exercise common sense; when it
feels right and you feel supported in your choice, these are good
signs that you have found the right teacher for you.

When the student is ready, the teacher appears! Practice patience, and as the saying goes, "good things come to those who
wait."

Reiki and Money

'There's a certain Buddhist calm that comes from having...
money in the bank.'

— TOM ROBBINS

The issue of charging money for Reiki can be a touchy subject for
many. Much of our western conditioning around spiritual traditions supports the way of the spiritual martyr, and that it isn't
spiritual to make a living from teaching or giving Reiki to others.
In many eastern traditions, particularly in the monastic tradition of

Southern Buddhism, living by donation is a way of life and this works well because the community is geared towards supporting this.

In the West, it's another story as these ideas are far from western peoples concepts. When people think of a donation, instead of giving $50 for a Reiki treatment, they will pull out of their purse a few small coins. This is ok if you do not rely upon your healing sessions as a source of income. If you do on the other hand, you may find this method could soon find you approaching your bank manager for a personal loan, just to pay the bills!

Another way to look at it is we cannot put a price on the Reiki energy itself, but it is important to place a price on our time. For if we had not invested our time and money to learn Reiki we would not have this service to offer to others in the first place.

It is important that some form of exchange occur. For some, the exchange is in the form of money, for others it is in the form of a material exchange and for others still it comes in the form of exchanging for services.

Some of the reasons why people feel uncomfortable charging money for Reiki often stems from feelings of deep-seated unworthiness. Other reasons come from the idea that anything spiritual should be for free and should in no way attract a fee. As if money could somehow taint the spiritual experience. These ideas hold no basis. Even in eastern societies there is always an exchange, whether this be in the form of a donation or money or goods and services from a benefactor. A teacher or practitioner of Reiki requires support for their time and expertise. Money is required for the teacher or practitioner to continue providing teachings, healing and energy.

If we spend our time giving a beneficial service to another, there must be some form of exchange. If we neglect this role, we are not creating an opportunity for the very person we wish to heal to give something back. In a way this is actually fostering an unbalanced relationship and a karmic debt for our client. Creating a space for exchange places a value on the service we offer and it is then appreciated and respected by the person we are treating. This is the most beneficial way to work for all concerned.

Just in the same way one should not undercharge, one should not overcharge. This too creates a negative karmic debt, but for the person setting the fee. The exchange should be based on the clients' ability to pay as well as setting a fee that is suitable for the services rendered.

In a modern world we must contemplate the value we place on

things. How many of us consider the money we pay for clothing, or a new CD, or a night out on the town? How many of us on a whim make the decision to purchase one or a number of consumer items, yet when it comes to purchasing the skills or training of a practitioner who could really benefit our lives, we still go through the: "should I or shouldn't I?"

One of the greatest investments one can make in this life is to invest in the health of our body and mind. All material things are impermanent and subject to decay. All things are in constant motion and we as human beings are subject to old age, sickness and death. If we set aside our desires and wants and allow ourselves to give in the spirit of generosity, we open the door to genuine prosperity and that is the richness of the human spirit.

CHAPTER FIVE

*'Your work is to find out what your work should be
and not to neglect it. Clearly discover your work and
attend to it with all your heart.'*

— THE DHAMMAPADA

Other Applications of Reiki

Reiki for Pregnancy

It is a great blessing for an expectant mother, family and friends to receive Reiki during a pregnancy. There have been many documented positive experiences where Reiki has been particularly helpful in pregnancy and especially during labor.

Reiki is also very beneficial in alleviating some of the common symptoms associated with pregnancy, such as lower back pain, swelling, poor circulation, and in the earlier stages, morning sickness.

Daily or weekly treatments are very beneficial for mother and baby, and it is usually suggested that the woman receive the four Reiki I attunements so she may give herself and her child Reiki whenever needed.

Giving the Reiki attunements to a pregnant woman is completely safe and acts as an additional blessing for the infant. Many pregnant women have attended Reiki workshops, and as a result have incorporated Reiki as part of their own self-healing and personal maintenance throughout their term. With the Mother giving Reiki to the unborn infant, there is a direct transmission of healing energy and love. This can only benefit both concerned, because, as the mother is giving Reiki to the infant in her womb, she is also transmitting healing energy to herself. In the past, some teachers of Reiki have stressed the concern that Reiki might cause a miscarriage in the first three months of pregnancy. The reason for this

contra-indication to the use of Reiki is not that it could in any way
contribute to a miscarriage, but for the reason that a practitioner
via association could be blamed and sued should this naturally
occur. Reiki of course is always safe and this contra-indication is
not due to any harm being caused; rather it is a means to protect
practitioners from potential legal action.

Sadly, many confuse this and think that Reiki can cause a miscarriage in the first three months of pregnancy and therefore refuse
to treat pregnant women. It is a great shame to neglect the use of
Reiki during this very special time. We should also consider that
Reiki is flowing all the time, therefore if a woman had learned
Reiki prior to pregnancy, and if this contra-indication were true,
then the number of miscarriages would increase exponentially.
Therefore, the use of Reiki during pregnancy is no cause for concern and can only assist as a sound support for both mother and
baby.

After the birth of a child, Reiki can also be very effective in healing the trauma associated with birth. Some mothers have also been
known to give Reiki to their breasts or breast milk as the child is
feeding, transmitting healing energy into the milk. Beyond the benefits of being breastfed, the child receives milk that is charged with
pure life force energy and love. Reiki is also an invaluable tool for
related problems in infancy, such as teething, irregular sleeping
patterns (both for parents and child), feeding problems and other
related problems in the early stages of development. So Reiki
should be used freely and frequently during this time.

Reiki has also been known to assist in fertility problems by
regularly directing healing energy to the sexual organs. This can be
either facilitated by one's partner, or as a self-treatment procedure.

Reiki for Children

When we look at facilitating Reiki on children, the major difference
is size. Having a smaller body to work on, the session's time may
decrease. As we all know, unless a child is quite ill, they will find it
difficult to remain still for extended periods of time and this becomes clear when they become irritable or start to squirm.

One of the best ways to give your child Reiki is when they are
going to sleep, or when they are asleep. In addition to this, absent
healing is another alternative to settling fears and other related
emotional states. Reiki can also be effective for children experiencing nightmares. Using a simple guided meditation, which incorporates Reiki, is an effective way to settle childhood fears. *(See chapter
10 on absent healing)*

Attuning Children to Reiki

Giving Reiki attunements to a child, no matter what age, is very beneficial as it teaches a child from an early age to gain self-reliance and self-love. It is perhaps one of the greatest gifts one could give.

A child can be attuned to Reiki at any age. However, for a child to sit still for a physical attunement, they need to be at an age where they will.

At the International Institute for Reiki Training (IIRT), we have had children as young as nine years of age who have participated in a Reiki I class accompanied by a parent. At this age, they do not take all the information in; however, this is also the case for most adults. So it is suggested that the child reviews the course a few years later to further the understanding and integrate the techniques and practices on a deeper level.

For children under the age of ten, the attunements are usually facilitated outside of a class environment. Here the parent or guardian acts as a mentor in the basic healing procedures. When the child is ready or is mature enough, we invite them to participate in a Reiki I class to formalize their training.

Attunements can be facilitated with the child present, or as an absent initiation procedure. As an absent procedure, the results remain the same and this practice is especially good for babies, toddlers and smaller children.

Reiki for Animals

Most domestic animals love Reiki and will often sit still long enough to receive what they require. The idea is not to force an animal to sit still, because animals are very intuitive and instinctual and know what they need in terms of receiving energy. This also works especially well for animals who are sick or dying. There are many Reiki practitioners amongst Veterinarians and other related animal health care professionals. Many of these practitioners report how the basic Reiki practices enhance the healing rate and calm the animals being treated. Reiki works especially well for animals that are distressed or injured. If the animal does not wish to be handled due to an injury, a distant healing procedure can be applied with the same, if not better, results. Another way to work is to place the hands above the specific area and to beam the Reiki energy.

The use of Flower essences and Bach Flower remedies such as Rescue Remedy are also very useful for distressed or injured animals. One of the best ways to apply the essence is to mix this into their food or drinking water or even to place a few drops on an area they will lick. One can also charge the essence with Reiki before applying it, to infuse Reiki energy into the medicine.

The trick is to be creative with Reiki and to give the animal how ever much it needs. You will soon know when they have received enough energy as they will simply get up and leave. Some animals, like cats and dogs who are accustomed to regular Reiki treatments will often become your best clients and will expect regular Reiki sessions. So be prepared to attend to the needs of your furry friends and you will be lavished with affection for your efforts.

Reiki and Dreaming

As we are becoming aware, Reiki is not limited by our thoughts or our state of Consciousness. So it is with sleep. On an average we spend more than a third of our lives asleep, and the good news is that we can facilitate Reiki on ourselves while sleeping. As stated previously, Reiki is activated by touch and does not require our conscious effort to make it happen. When we are sleeping and have our hands in contact either with ourselves or someone else, healing energy is being transmitted.

Simply placing our hands 'on' is not only a great way to 'nod off' but it is also a useful time to work on our own self-healing. After a short time our hands naturally end up on our body, and during our sleep we can receive much healing. Reiki is also a useful technique for those who have trouble falling asleep. I once had a client who had averaged one or two hours a night for the last twenty years. After attending the Reiki beginners' class and receiving the attunements, she reported the next day that for the very first time, she had slept a good eight hours. With regular self-healing treatments each evening in bed, she continued to have deep and restful sleep, which had a considerable positive impact on her life.

Reiki is also a self-help technique for people who have irregular sleeping patterns. As soon as you wake up, begin the self-healing and in no time at all, you will be back in the land of nod.

It is also common for Reiki practitioners to experience heightened dream activity as a result of initiation and continued Reiki practice.

Research shows that individuals who are deprived of Alpha sleep have poor productivity during the day. (*Alpha describes a measurement of Brain waves relating to creative states, deep awareness and relaxation. It should be noted that the common state of consciousness of a practitioner facilitating Reiki is in the Alpha state of consciousness. The Alpha state is also the stage one enters at the tail end of active dreamtime during the night.)*

Whenever we are facilitating Reiki on others or ourselves, we naturally access the Alpha state and are therefore in a highly creative, vigilant and healing state of mind.

Our brains cannot help but be in this state of consciousness, which promotes healing, inspiration and personal insights. With regular nightly reminders to place our hands on our body, we can begin to form a life long habit of nocturnal healing that brings with it a renewed vitality and energy each morning.

Reiki for Meditation

'Reiki is Wisdom and Truth.'

— HAWAYO TAKATA

When a person is facilitating or receiving Reiki, the most common state of consciousness measured is the Alpha Level. Deep meditative and creative flow is associated with the Alpha level. So whenever you are giving or receiving Reiki, you are in fact in a state conducive to meditation. This is great news for those people who say they cannot meditate. For when you give Reiki you are in the state of mind that is meditation.

Reiki takes you to a still point. This is a place of deep awareness. With regular practice these moments increase to a point where one simply abides in a peaceful state of mind.

Many people report a deep sense of peace and stillness as a result of Reiki. This still point is a place of non-doing.

Meditation spans a variety of forms, and it is not simply about sitting in full lotus position and saying OM every 10 minutes. Meditation can be a walk in nature, doing something you are completely engaged in, making love, or anything that brings you into the present moment where you are highly aware and awake in your mind. The more you do Reiki, the more peaceful you will become. With long-term practice, your mind will come to know stillness, not as an unusual experience but as a daily state of mind.

Although it is not completely necessary to have full awareness for Reiki to work, a state of meditation naturally begins to manifest more and more with regular practice. For people who regularly meditate, and who have received the Reiki attunements, a greater enhancement to meditation practice is found and one is often more able to sustain longer periods of stillness and awareness.

One can also incorporate Reiki into a meditation practice. There are many techniques and practices. One of the simplest ways is to give yourself a self-healing treatment and hold awareness on the transference of healing energy at each point. The point of the meditation is to train the mind to be present on sensation within the area of contact as ones progresses throughout the body.

Reiki and Group Healing

In addition to your regular hands on healing treatments, group Reiki is a wonderful extension. This is where there can be more than one person facilitating Reiki on another. There is no worry of overloading a person with group healing. One can liken it to a glass being filled by several streams at once. As a result the healing time is significantly decreased.

With group hands on healing we are in effect doubling our capacity to heal with an additional practitioner. This capacity increases with each additional practitioner. Now this does not necessarily make Reiki better if there are more practitioners. The difference is that we are simply working in a wider capacity and transmitting healing energy at a faster rate.

Reiki comes from the highest intelligence. From this source, Reiki goes to wherever it is needed, providing healing to the degree the individual can comfortably assimilate.

In a group healing, the practitioners place their hands in the positions of major energy flow. For example, one at the sides of the head, one at the upper chest, one at the lower abdomen and one practitioner at the feet. Working in this way enhances the amount of life force transmitted into the body and energy field of the recipient.

It is not uncommon to feel the subtle reverberations of a healing extend for days or even weeks. Though what people experience in a Reiki treatment varies tremendously.

Another extension to group healing is group distant healing. In a similar fashion to group healing, a collective stream of healing energy transfers to another. The difference is that the healing energy is sent at a distance over time and space.

How to Let Go with Reiki

When we receive the Reiki I initiation we are bringing a considerable amount of universal energy into our lives, so it makes sense to do a little 'spring clean'. Although the following methods are not traditionally a part of Reiki, the 'letting go' ritual focuses on releasing our limiting beliefs and views about our lives. In this process we write on a piece of paper all the parts of ourselves that no longer serve our paths. Through this process we put a signal out to the universe, which states that we are willing to let go in order to become more of who we truly are.

Letting Go Procedure: Part 1

Write on a piece of paper all the things that no longer serve you and your life path. Give thanks for the lessons that these things have given you, and state in your mind that you no longer want these in your life. Include situations and people you wish to forgive.

At the end of your list, write: *"I now choose to release these things back to the Universe for the highest good of all concerned."*

Hold the statements written between your hands. Now imagine all of these statements as symbols or objects residing in your body. Imagine these objects leaving your body and going into the paper between your hands. Once you feel this is complete, give a prayer for the lessons you have learned, and blow a short sharp breath between your hands. (This symbolizes the release of these issues.)

When you have completed this process, burn the page in a bowl of sand.

Now imagine that your body is completely cleansed by the Reiki energy as a shower of healing energy descends upon you. This cleanses any remnants of these from your body and mind.

How to Manifest with Reiki

Manifestation Procedure: Part 2

Write on a piece of paper all the things you wish to manifest in your life. Include situations that will serve your path and anyone's name that you feel requires healing. Give thanks for your life and the many gifts you have. At the end of your list, write: *"I now choose to manifest all of these things into my life, not only for my highest good, but for the highest good of all concerned. This or something better comes to me now."*

Hold the paper close to your body and imagine that all of these qualities are coming into your body in the form of positive symbols and objects. Once you feel this is complete, offer a prayer of thanks for your life and for the opportunity to become more of your true essence.

Once you have completed this process, burn the page in a bowl of sand. (We burn our manifestations to release our attachment to the outcome.)

Closing Procedure: Part 3

Take the ashes to a place in nature, such as the ocean, a hill or place that is special for you. Cast some of the ashes to the winds of each of the four directions, East, North, West and South, in an anti-clockwise direction.

Call all those who would help in this process, from each direction. Once the four directions have been completed, call this from above and lastly from the earth itself.

Give a final prayer of thanks for the gifts you already have in your life, and dedicate these gifts to the benefit of all that lives. Place the remaining ashes where you stand as a marker of the occasion. This completes the ritual.

This procedure is extremely effective and one will often see results. You can repeat these procedures once a month, or whenever you are feeling stuck or blocked in your life. Remember not to put fixed outcomes in your prayers or affirmations. Leave it open-ended to allow the universe to bring this to you in the path of least resistance.

The use of Reiki in Daily Life

We can see that Reiki has numerous applications to numerous situations.

Because Reiki is as simple as placing ones hands on oneself or another, the applications are many and varied. Incorporating Reiki into daily life is as easy as remembering that your hands have a new role to play. A little Reiki each day is better than none at all. So with this in mind, here are some helpful tips to incorporate hands on healing each day.

Give yourself Reiki:

- While watching TV, or send absent healing to a specific issue.
- While driving your car (when a hand is free) or when you are a passenger.
- While relaxing.
- After finishing a meal, by placing your hands on your stomach and intestines to aid in the digestion of your food.
- When walking in nature or anywhere for that matter.
- When going to sleep.

- Whenever you have a physical complaint or stress in your body.
- Whenever you have either one or both hands free.

Even if you can only do five minutes a day there is always a connection and some benefit. It is about learning to remember that your hands are now tools for your personal empowerment. We can apply this simple principle to almost anything we can conceive. It is not necessary to limit the ways or the times in which we use Reiki. Reiki energy is as creative and diverse as you are. Test the boundaries and see where it takes you. There can be no harm caused using the energy alone, so as long as your personal motivation is pure, it can only lead to new and improved experiences.

Moving forward in this way, the Divine intelligence of Reiki will meet you half way, teaching and supporting you in your journey. All you need to do is begin it now!

CHAPTER SIX

'Scriptures say that both wisdom lacking means
and means lacking wisdom are bondage.
Therefore do not abandon either.'

— ATISA, BODHIPATHAPRADIPA

Healing and the Cause of Illness

When we look at what it means to be healed, different questions come to mind. Does this merely involve the removal of physical afflictions or does it go deeper? Healing not only encompasses the physical being; it encompasses the whole of our consciousness. It is worth considering not only our current symptoms, but the cause of illness as well.

Current research tells us that most modern diseases are caused by stress, poor diet and a poor personal self-image. From a Reiki perspective the cause of illness goes much deeper. Certainly stress, diet and self-image have an effect on our health, yet this is not the primary cause of illness. We might pose the question then: Why do we get sick? The primary reason is due to previous karma's ripening in our present situation. The things we have done, thought and said contribute to our present situation. We can do much to purify these negative karmas by regularly attending to our healing. A very direct way is by ceasing to continue negative actions and to replace these with positive actions. Other factors are due to wrong views; wrong actions; wrong speech; and wrong livelihood. We need to carefully examine all areas of our lives and see how we can change these to positive actions.

On an energy level, negative actions cause a disharmonious vibration in our energy field. Our energy field can also become misaligned by choosing to live in poisoned environments, with negative people, and by engaging in negative thoughts as well as the kinds of substances we choose to ingest. So we must do our best to purify these imbalances and to bring back a harmonious balance. Self-healing is a direct way to re-align oneself. Giving up harmful actions is another.

The Historical Buddha gives some useful guidelines for a balanced life. One set of famous teachings is **The Eightfold Noble Path**. These eight teachings are set out as the ways to take a person away from sorrow. If we choose to follow these guidelines we are more able to be free from disturbing emotions and wrong views. It is said by following these eight steps one gains steady insight into the nature of their mind. With careful attention and practice, the Buddha taught that these eight steps bring about four sublime states – benevolence, compassion, sympathetic joy and equanimity.

The Eightfold Noble Path is set out as follows:

1. The first being the path of *Right View*: Without a proper understanding into the nature of our problems we can do little to remedy the cause. Therefore we should strive to know the nature of our minds, recognize the nature of reality and closely examine our motives and needs. By understanding the Four Noble Truths which are: the truth of suffering, the origin of suffering, the way beyond suffering, and the way of The Eightfold Noble Path, we have the view to understanding the non-individuality of all existence. Right view then is ultimately reduced to an understanding of the four noble truths.

2. The second is the path of *Right Thought*. It matters how we think. Many of our present thoughts are based on confusion, misunderstanding and prejudice. Therefore one should strive to follow a path of right action, including good will to others, thoughts of love and non-violence, and not harming sentient beings. The path of virtuous thoughts can do much to undo our conditioned minds and to generate the heart of wisdom.

3. The third path is that of *Right Speech*. To recognize the value of non-harmful speech and therefore avoid lying, slander and gossip. Instead one nurtures communication, which is friendly, benevolent, meaningful and life giving. This includes the speech we say in our own minds about others and ourselves.

4. The fourth path is that of *Correct Conduct*. To avoid actions that are in conflict with the cultivation of ethical and moral behavior. Therefore one avoids destroying life, from taking that which is not freely given, dishonest dealings and sexual promiscuity. Thus we strive to be mindful of how we conduct ourselves in a manner that is not only ethical but reflects how we can nurture

this in others to lead an honorable and peaceful life.

5. The fifth path is the path of *Right Livelihood*. To recognize the importance of a livelihood that supports the path of unfolding. It matters what we do, therefore one should avoid a vocation that causes harm to either ourselves, another or the environment.

6. The sixth path is the path of *Right Effort*. To bring conscious effort into all that we do. This path represents the will to prevent unwholesome states of mind from arising. Instead one cultivates wholesome thoughts and nurtures a mind that causes good thoughts to arise. With a sound motivation and intention to bring the right effort into our minds, we bring out our best and steadily progress upon the path of peace.

7. The seventh path is the path of *Right Mindfulness*. This path includes attention to the needs of our body, sensations and feelings, ideas, thoughts and concepts, and the activities of the emotions and mind. With proper awareness one is in control of one's actions. One is also more present and we can see how things really are, and not giving into expectations and projections from the past or future.

8. The eighth path is the path of *Right Concentration*. This is the training of the mind through mediation. By bringing concentrated effort to the mind for the practice of meditation, one is able to recognize the way things are and to achieve 'one pointed' focus that results in a calm and tranquil mind.

Considering these teachings and living them can do much to cease our present sorrows as well as sowing the seeds of future negative karmas. Reiki touches every part of our being, therefore, the more we practice Reiki the greater capacity we have for health and balance. It is in this way that many begin a healing path, either as a practitioner offering this service to others or simply to a lesser degree through regular self-healing. The ideal situation is a perfect balance of both, yet one must start at a level that is practical for ones current situation. This way you can start where you are and not where your Ego would imagine yourself to be.

Reiki and Allopathic Medicine

As described in previous sections, Reiki can be used on the physical level to complement conventional allopathic medicine. Reiki is becoming more and more popular amongst general practitioners, in hospitals and hospice-care. Because Reiki energy speeds the body's natural ability to heal itself we find the use of Reiki for healing physical ailments an excellent example. Reiki is also a wonderful method of pain management. Its regular use can do much to reduce chronic pain in most cases and reduce pain symptoms with regular treatments.

It is important to note here that Reiki does not subscribe to being a sole method of healing, but rather a complementary method which when used in conjunction with other therapies can greatly assist in the rate of healing. A recipient of a Reiki treatment should in no way reduce or cease any medication or ignore the recommendations of a qualified health professional.

Many doctors who have taken Reiki training can use hands on during treatments to reduce pain or calm patients who are experiencing anxiety. It has also been determined that Reiki can alter the negative effects of some drugs used in cancer treatment and other serious illnesses. Reiki is also very popular among nurses and workers in the mental health field for comforting patients who are in fear or emotional pain. At the IIRT we have had a number of General Practitioners, nurses and mental health practitioners who have all contested to the enormous benefits of Reiki within their own practice, and in their personal self-healing.

Another way to use Reiki with conventional medicine is to charge medicines with Reiki energy. Simply holding the medication in your hands for 10 minutes before taking it can make a noticeable difference. It is also a good idea to energize other medications as well as herbs to enhance their healing properties.

Factors Determining Wellness

In conjunction with 'hands-on' sessions it is worthy to note some of the other factors that contribute to health and well-being. Most of these ideas are based on common sense, but many of us do not consider these when we are ill or unbalanced in our lives. What we eat, how and where we sleep and the company we keep all determine the rate of healing. The following are some guidelines that anyone can utilize when ill or when caring for a patient.

The Environment of an Ill Person

When we are ill, there is a tendency to go inward, to block out natural light and withdraw from others. This is not only a rapid way to become depressed, it is a sure recipe for remaining ill. So the environment of a room is very important in promoting health. The room of the patient should be well lit with natural light, preferably not fluorescent lighting, as well as being well ventilated. Ventilation should be from a natural source and not regulated by air-conditioning. The best option is an open window, provided one does not live on a busy and polluted highway.

An ordered room, which is uncluttered, will also enhance positive energies. To enhance the elements of nature in a room is also a great benefit. Providing indoor plants and flowers are subconscious symbols of life and vitality, and can also enhance the energy of a room and the overall mood of a patient.

Having a symbol of aspiration or inspiration in the room again works on the unconscious mind to promote healing. If the person is religious, then an image to represent their belief system or an image of nature where the individual has a continual view will assist in recovery and will soothe the mind.

Playing soothing and gentle music also enhances the rate of healing and should be incorporated with 'hands on' sessions to set an ambient mood.

Burning high quality incense or clearing the room from any negative energies discharged can also be of benefit.

Clothing and bedding also hold energy, so if a person has a fever and is sweating out toxins, they are literally lying in their own toxins. Changing clothing everyday and bedding every second day will clear excess build-up of lower vibrational energy.

The Element of Water and our Physical Direction

Over 80% of our body is composed of the element water, and as we know, the moon affects the tides by its directional movement from the east to the west. In keeping with this concept, it makes sense to approach our spiritual practices, and even the direction in which we sleep, to flow with the cycles of the moon. Our internal waters are affected directly by this movement, so having your bed facing the axis of east/west will enhance balance. This is heightened with regards to an ill person who is trying to recover. When we face the northern direction, because our water is out of sync, it makes us tense; when we face the southern direction, it makes us weak. It is important to sleep with your head facing either the east or west axis. In this way we are staying in tune with the cycles of nature and the flow of universal energy.

Exercise

Many would consider exercise the last thing on their mind when they are ill; however, light exercise and being outside when the weather permits, is a vital element to health and wellness.

Participating in low-impact exercise such as short gentle walks is generally best. However, it is vitally important that the indi-

vidual does not become overly hot or cool and is sufficiently maintained at an acceptable temperature, only doing the amount of exercise they can manage. To overdo it, can lead to a worsening of
their condition. When possible choose to walk in nature. Simply
being in a natural setting where the life force is abundant tends to
rub off on an ill person and will enhance their physical and mental
well-being. A good routine is to walk for a comfortable time, then
sit in meditation in a natural environment, and then walk again.
This routine enhances balance and awareness. Engaging in other
exercises that cultivate the enhancement of vital energy such as Tai
Chi or Chi Kung are also of great benefit.

   Another beneficial and pleasurable extension to this is sexual
intercourse. If the patient's strength permits, and the person is not
suffering from any sexually transmitted or communicable diseases,
then sexual congress should be allowed and even encouraged. The
act of lovemaking is extremely beneficial in releasing the body's
natural endorphins and this aids in the patients general mood, relaxation and overall happiness.

Diet, Alcohol, Drugs and Healing

It makes sense to attend to a diet that is balanced with the five food
groups with particular emphasis on fresh, organic and 'Chi' orien-
tated foods. Fresh food is packed with life force that translates directly to you when you consume it. It should go without saying
that recreational drugs and alcohol do not mix with illness. These
substances directly affect the fragile life force of the sick person. At
no time should a person who is ill use recreational drugs or alcohol
as a form of escape. This does nothing for the advancement of healing in the body and the replenishment of vital energy. Of course,
this does not mean that one should cease their prescribed medication from a General Practitioner. However if you are so inclined,
giving Reiki to your medication before taking it can enhance the
positive qualities of the medicine.

Keeping the Right Company, a Positive Outlook

Keeping the right company when you are ill is helpful in maintaining a positive outlook and the advancement of personal esteem
and balance. The last thing you need when you are ill is someone
else telling you all about his or her problems and filling your mind
with concerns and worry. It is a general rule to avoid people and
situations that are filled with negative views. This has particular
emphasis when someone is ill. The power of positive thinking has

been well documented in relation to enhancing health and activating healing energies in the body. If you are confined to a bed with your illness, read or have someone read books to you that are inspirational and motivated toward a positive outlook. Likewise watch films that are of a similar nature. What we put into our bodies and mind greatly influences our outlook and view of life.

Incorporating Other Modalities

Reiki is not the only form of alternative medicine that can assist when we are out of balance. It is a good idea to incorporate other modalities that you feel may help your situation. Some other alternative methods such as Chinese herbs, massage, shiatsu, acupuncture, naturopathy, reflexology, homeopathy, flower essence therapy and aromatherapy are all excellent approaches to healing and well-being. However, just as it is with Reiki, be certain that the practitioner is fully trained and competent in their art before investing your time, health and money. Combining Reiki with these modalities greatly enhances them in a variety of ways. For example, in most forms of bodywork practitioners have their hands in contact with the recipient's body most of the time. As Reiki is activated by touch, healing energy is being transmitted via the hands directly into the meridians, organs, muscles and energy system of the individual. In homeopathy, aromatherapy and flower essence therapy Reiki can enhance the positive healing qualities of the remedies by holding the medicine in your hands and energizing them with the Reiki energy.

Preventative Medicine

The best approach to wellness is not to get sick in the first place. If we pay attention to our physical bodies, our mental, and our emotional needs, we prevent the causes of illness. Applying some of the preceding suggestions will certainly assist in this process. Good health is mostly common sense and listening to the wisdom of your body. Following these guidelines in conjunction with regular Reiki self-treatment enhances a positive outlook and creates balance physically, emotionally, and mentally. So many people are unhappy in their work and with their relationships and feel that it is their lot in life to remain in an unsatisfying job for many years. For some, life is just about work, to then retire and then expire. Following your dreams and passions is so important to living well and creating happiness. With continued use of Reiki and by attending to some of the suggestions previously outlined, we can open the door to a better outlook for our health and life in general. Most importantly, do what you love to do.

If we are unhappy, is it due to outer influences or are we manifesting negative situations through our own co-creation? If something is not right, do what you can to change it. If our situation is too difficult to work out, take time to seek counseling from a qualified therapist. If we need distance from our situation, a short retreat can also be useful. Just remember, 'the only Zen that you find on top of the mountain is the Zen you took with you'. You have all the resources you need. Tap this power and use it to the best of your ability. We can do much to change our situations in life. We have a choice.

Reiki for First aid

First and foremost, Reiki is not designed to replace common sense and basic first aid procedures. However, Reiki is an excellent adjunct to first aid. For example, if someone has cut himself or herself, one can apply a bandage and at the same time hold the area with our hands, transferring Reiki energy. To be most affective in a first aid situation, it is suggested to start applying the Reiki energy as soon as possible. The sooner we apply Reiki to the affected area, the sooner we are preventing unnecessary trauma from setting in. If it is not possible to place the hands in the affected area we can use the law of correspondence via Absent Healing. See chapter 10.

Here we state that the part we are holding corresponds to the affected area, and imagine healing energy going to that place. At the Reiki I level, we simply place our hands wherever we can and state in our minds that the area we are touching now corresponds to the area in need. In addition to this, we can visualize this area beneath our hands as the affected area. Where possible we leave our hands in the area as long as is comfortably possible for the person concerned. This may require you to be working on the area for a number of hours. Working in this way will greatly enhance the recovery and healing of the individual. It also makes a lot of sense to learn basic first aid. Courses are widely available and are an essential adjunct to any practitioner of the healing arts.

Practice and Support

To further your relationship with Reiki, it is essential to put it into daily practice. Reiki works on the premise, like most things, that the more you put into it, the more you'll get back. So it makes sense to create the situations and time in your life to make this possible.

What helps tremendously with practice is the support from like-minded friends on the path. Many Reiki schools hold regular 'Reiki Share' evenings, as well as Reiki healing clinics and opportunities to review previous levels. This helps to strengthen and reconnect bonds made with old friends and to form new friendships. Most importantly groups like this give you the opportunity to practice with others who are interested in healing.

If the teacher you learn from does not offer practice times or ongoing support after the workshop, then take a leap of faith and contact other teachers and practitioners in your area to swap sessions. So often, the detriment of an individuals practice is due to the lack of support from like-minded people on the path. When we isolate ourselves, we potentially limit our growth. This is why it is recommended to learn Reiki with a spouse, close friend, brother or sister, so that one can support the other in creating a space for practice.

Practical Practice

When we look at all of the various kinds of therapies, courses and workshops available today, it is often exciting to taste all these kinds of experiences. Yet if a teaching or method has no practical application in your life, what use is it? It becomes all too easy to collect Certificates and to attend every workshop under the sun, but without proper integration and right understanding, we may just be filling our heads with lots of information without putting any of it to use.

Engaging your mind with sensational phenomena may be entertaining but how does it contribute to healing? The following story illustrates this, and how one's practice should benefit not only oneself, but also others in a practical and grounded way.

The following is a story from Buddha's time to illustrate this point.

In India there was a Sadhu or Holy man who through many years of practice had learned to walk on water. One day, Buddha was walking along the river and met the Sadhu.

The Sadhu, not recognizing Buddha as an awakened being, tried to impress him with his magical abilities.

The Sadhu performed many magical feats, such as levitating, manifesting colorful energy fields, small objects and the like.

Each time he performed an act, the Buddha would respond with enthusiasm, and would say: "That is amazing, what else can you do?"

Seeing that the Buddha was so impressed, the Sadhu saved his greatest act till last.

"I can walk across this river", he exclaimed, literally bursting with pride, and proceeded to walk on water. Buddha, seeing a boat nearby, rowed the river and reached the other side. Once there he spoke to the Sadhu asking him how long it had taken him to accomplish this great feat. The Sadhu said, "It has taken me thirty years to achieve this act!" Buddha said, "Wow!, thirty years to do that, it took me five minutes in that boat, what else can you do?"

At this point the Sadhu recognized the futility of his practice by the profound example of the Buddha to awaken his mind to practices that have a benefit for others. He later became an avid follower of the Buddha's teachings and dedicated the rest of his life to the practical pursuit of awakening, grounded in the service and healing of all beings.

— POPULAR BUDDHIST FABLE, SOURCE UNKNOWN

So a teaching is of little worth if it does not liberate oneself or others. We should closely examine our minds and be honest with ourselves. Our motivation for becoming a healer should be based on the compassionate wish to benefit others. These days there are many vehicles to the spiritual path, so be sure the path you embark upon bears results. If we waste our time pursuing spiritual teachings that are shrouded in mystery and blind belief, we are hardly developing self-reliance, compassion and healing. A spiritual teaching that teaches you to find your own awakening is a path worth pursuing. Buddha said, "Learn to do good, cease to do harm, and purify your mind. By these actions, follow the teachings of the Awakened and be a light unto yourself".

Practice Requirements for First Degree

Having completed a Reiki First Degree workshop, it is suggested to complete a self-healing session every day for a period of 21 days. The reason for this is by the end of 21 days you would have formed a good habit and will be more able to naturally continue. It is also suggested that a new student complete at least 30 hours of Reiki hands on healing treatments on family and friends before considering Reiki Second Degree. If you practice the recommended hours you will greatly enhance your understanding and integration of the First Degree training.

21 Days Integration

It is said that having completed a Reiki I workshop, there is a 3-

week period of integration. This is not really such a strange concept, when we consider that our entire energetic system has had a complete enhancement and realignment with the four Reiki attunements. During this time it is best to be aware of how the energy is shaping you. Many people report that they feel considerably different after a workshop and in the weeks that follow. Your personal experience is your own, and often you feel these changes on an emotional and mental level. Common experiences range from a deeper sense of peace and serenity to inner calm and greater clarity. Many people report that once they have experienced the attunements in the workshop environment, the stresses of daily life don't seem to take hold or hold as much focus as previously experienced.

It is also suggested to nurture oneself during this period, and to pay attention to our bodies' needs.

One of the most effective ways to integrate the Reiki energy is to give yourself a daily self-treatment. Doing this greatly enhances your direct perception of the Reiki energy and allows the balancing of your physical, emotional, psychological and spiritual bodies. There are many benefits of daily practice. As we work on a daily level, we effectively build on previous sessions and as a result the degree of clearing, heightened sensitivity and one's perception becomes more enhanced. Sometimes emotions can arise as a result of regular practice. The important thing to remember is that it is all part of the healing process, and although it may not be very pleasant at the time, it is actually a good sign. Often, if this is occurring, it is the mind's way of signaling some breakthrough of an old dysfunctional pattern. It is best to continue self-healing especially when this is unfolding, as it will assist in the transition and healing taking place.

It is also good to have a friend or therapist to help if you are processing many emotions. Sometimes it can help a great deal when we talk about our problems with someone else. Even if they just listen, that can be enough.

Keeping a Reiki Journal

Many people take up the suggestion of keeping a personal Reiki journal, to document their experiences and changes in themselves. Engaging in this process can be quite rewarding and acts as a marker in times of transition. It may also simply off-load what's on your mind. Keeping a journal is a way to reflect on your personal growth and the changes that have occurred in your life as a result of your practice. If you decide to keep a regular Reiki journal, take note of your experiences and how you felt during your treatments. Also take notes on your clients' experiences and remember to ask for feedback when you are learning. You may also wish to create a client feedback book or page and ask your client to give some comments at the end of each session. Feedback can be an excellent source and can tell you much about your Reiki ability and development as a practitioner.

Requirements for a First Degree Workshop

Each teacher of Reiki brings their own unique teaching style and approach when passing on their understanding of the system. This of course is fine as people are varied in the way they learn and grow. Perhaps this is also a reason for the many and varied Reiki styles emerging in the west. Although Reiki styles differ from one teacher to the next, in general some basic things should be covered during a First Degree Reiki workshop. The following are some general guidelines to keep in mind.

1. Four Reiki Attunements. Two each day, either morning and afternoon or one each day over four consecutive days.
2. Students are shown traditional hand positions, and have the opportunity to practice at least two separate Reiki sessions within the workshop environment.
3. Students have an opportunity to explore intuitive approaches to hands on healing.
4. Students are shown the application of calling in the Reiki energy, centering procedures, how to create personal boundaries and related practices.
5. Students are told the Reiki History, the importance of lineage and where they fit into the Reiki Lineage.
6. Practice requirements are given during the workshop.
7. Students receive a manual of procedures and information on Reiki's applications.
8. Students receive a Certificate for First Degree Reiki once they have completed the necessary training requirements.
9. Total Workshop duration: Approximately 14 Hours.

CHAPTER SEVEN

'For the things we have to learn,
before we can learn them, we learn by doing them.'

— ARISTOTLE

Frequently Asked Questions

Q: *What makes Reiki unique from other healing modalities?*

A: Reiki is one of the few energy healing systems that does not require focused intent or specific mental imagery to create a positive result. Once someone has received the Reiki attunements, Reiki energy is activated by touch. When you think of all the energy systems around these days, one could draw an analogy of these systems to a hand. The palm of the hand represents the source of all things and the fingers represent the various forms of energy work. One finger is Reiki, another is Chi Kung, and another is Pranic Healing and so on. Just as a finger is different in appearance to a thumb, so Reiki is different to other healing traditions. All systems come from the same source, yet each one has its own unique expression, form and style. Another unique feature of this system is the source of the healing energy. Reiki does not come from one's own energy field. It comes through your energy system as a result of the Reiki attunements. It is a product of the interaction with Universal healing energy, and the individual's energy system. Few systems of healing work in a similar manner.

Q: *What do I think of when I'm doing Reiki; do I need to act in a certain way?*

A: At the Reiki for beginners level, we simply observe what we are sensing and that is all. With the higher Reiki levels there is a greater emphasis on visualization, however, at the first level a student uses methods to develop stillness while facilitating the transference of Universal energy. Once the Reiki attunements are in order, the healing energy is activated by touch, and this is why it is not necessary to concentrate to make it happen. By simply engaging in another's energy system or our own, the healing energy transfers.

In the words of Mrs. Takata: " Hands on – Reiki on, Hands off – Reiki off!"

Q: *Is it necessary to visualize anything while facilitating Reiki?*

A: At the Reiki I level, it is not a requirement to visualize anything to make it happen. As previously mentioned, the Reiki energy flows once the hands are within the energy field or on the body of the recipient. In the Reiki levels beyond First Degree, visualization can be incorporated into your sessions. This is achieved by visualizing symbols, which are given at the Second Degree. One utilizes these symbols for directing healing energy for specific situations. In addition to this, some practitioners like to visualize themselves as empty vessels for the energy to pass through or they may visualize the energy going to a particular part of the body of the recipient. However, this is not essential as the energy is already doing this by itself. These visualizations can assist as a means of focus for your own mind, by keeping attention and awareness on the task at hand. Just remember that it is the Divine Intelligence of Reiki doing the healing and not yourself.

Q: *Are abilities like clairvoyance, psychic ability and seeing auras a necessary part of Reiki?*

A: These sorts of phenomena are not essential to facilitate an effective Reiki treatment. The tools that are imparted in the attunement process awaken the stream of Universal healing energy from yourself to the recipient. With practice, some of these inner abilities naturally begin to arise. Each person tends to develop these abilities at a different rate, and it is largely dependant upon how much one practices and applies the methods taught at the various Reiki levels. Certainly, specific attunements in the levels also focus on the opening of the inner senses. So, it is a balance between your own inner unfolding that comes through practice and the attunements that open specific doorways of energy within the being on a clairvoyant level.

One should not be too concerned if you are or are not experiencing these sorts of phenomena. If you are, then that's okay and if not, then that is also okay. Reiki does not require any special talent or spiritual predisposition to achieve positive results. Remember, healing is the goal, not how psychic you are.

Q: *Once you have completed Reiki I, can you lose the healing energy or can it be taken away by a negative experience?*

A: Provided the recipient has received the four initiations in Reiki First Degree by a qualified teacher, the energy stays with the individual for the rest of their life. It can never be lost or hindered once the person has received these attunements. The Reiki attunements also create a protective quality within and around a person, and by simply facilitating Reiki, this protective quality manifests. Once the attunements are in place, it is like your Reiki antenna is locked on the Universal station and from that day forth you become a receiver of that station. Because Reiki is not a belief system, it is not subject to the projections or doubts from others or ourselves. In no way can Reiki be diminished. However, it can be enhanced through ongoing use and daily application.

Q: *Can everyone do Reiki?*

A: The Reiki initiations are a specific formula, which have a specific result. This result creates a pathway for transmitting the Reiki energy. This alignment always occurs, regardless of whether your personal belief is uncertain. It makes no difference if you believe in your ability. It makes no difference whether you believe in Reiki. The thing to know is the Divinity of Reiki believes in you. Put simply, if you have an energetic system (which everyone does) then you have what it takes to become a channel for Reiki energy.

Q: *If you are giving yourself Reiki and fall asleep, does the energy switch off?*

A: Reiki energy is not dependant on your state of consciousness. If the Reiki energy works without your thoughts and is activated by touch, then no matter what your state of consciousness, the healing will work regardless. I personally experienced this first hand one day when I received Reiki from one of my teachers. He had been working late and was very tired. As Reiki tends to create a space for what your body most needs he actually fell asleep while giving me Reiki. As he was snoring in my ear, which was quite amusing and disturbing, the Reiki energy was still flowing strongly through his hands. The good news is, you can get quite a lot of self-healing done when you are asleep.

Q: *Are some people better at Reiki than others?*

A: Some people have a natural pre-disposition to healing abilities and may be more attuned to subtle energies. However, even if you don't naturally have this, it can be developed once initiated. This sensitivity is also cultivated through on-going practice. Some people just develop this faster than others.

Q: *Are all the Reiki systems out there the same?*

A: No, not all Reiki systems offered are the same. As outlined in Chapter 1, there are many Reiki styles and the methods that accompany each style differ to a greater or lesser extent. Many teachers have also put their own ideas into Reiki and gradually the various forms of Reiki have changed. As a result, the passing of information and techniques does vary greatly from teacher to teacher. Naturally teachers bring their unique style to the Reiki system. Where a departure from traditional teachings occurs is when a teacher decides to remove or add elements to the symbols or initiations, which are essentially the foundation of the Reiki system. Some of the confusion regarding the different systems currently available is due to teachers being improperly trained. So it is important to find the right teacher who can give you the right transmission, methodology and teachings in order to achieve the best results.

Q: *Can Reiki Harm instead of heal?*

A: Of the many things on offer in the healing field, Reiki would have to be one of the most non-invasive and safest healing treatments. This is not only because receiving a treatment involves no manipulation of the physical body, it is also because the energy itself cannot cause an imbalance by either overuse or wrong application.

The practitioner simply places their hands gently on the body and the transference of healing energy passes via the hands to the recipient. Reiki brings about a calm and serene experience for both the giver and receiver.

The reason behind Reiki's safety is due to its non-dualistic vibration. It we look, for example at dualistic healing methods we could look at Chi energy. Chi energy refers to the raw life force energy and it is not the same in vibration as Reiki energy. For example, a martial arts expert can learn how to utilize Chi energy to strike a fatal blow to a person or a Chinese Qi Qgong Master might utilize the same energy with positive intent to heal an injury. It can be used for positive or not so positive means depending upon the practitioners' intention and belief.

Dualistic forms of energy are dependant upon the practitioners' intention, mental focus and depth of skill. However, in just the same way, these same energies can be switched to destructive purposes if intended in this way.

Reiki is a non-dualistic energy. In this way a practitioner does not need to believe in Reiki for Reiki to work. The practitioner does not need to focus their attention for it to transfer and if a practitioner has a negative thought or is in a troubled or an unbalanced state of mind, their thoughts will have no adverse effect upon the Reiki energy being transferred.

Q: *Is Reiki a Cult or Religion?*

A: Reiki is neither a Cult nor a Religion. The system certainly derives its base from Buddhism, yet in order to learn Reiki one does not need to prescribe to the Buddhist view of reality. The Reiki system known in the West is also not based on an individual dogma or structured belief system. However, it is a spiritual system that is experientially based and contains principles for gaining self-empowerment and personal development.

Q: *Does Reiki work every time?*

A: There is always some benefit when receiving a Reiki treatment. The degree of what is felt and healed varies from person to person. Some results can be life changing or in the miraculous category, while at other times it is an on-going and gradual process. Certainly there are noticeable benefits, such as relaxation and reduced stress. Reiki also provides immediate relief for a variety of aches and pains.

Q: *What is Absent healing?*

A: Absent healing is the ability to send healing energy at a distance. This method is taught in Second Degree. Absent healing is not bound by time, distance or space. With this ability we can assist in the positive outcomes to situations of the past, present or future. Absent healing methods can also heal others at a distance as well as heal various emotional issues. Just in the same way we can give our self, self-healing, so these same principles apply to absent healing. This method includes directing healing energy to areas of the body that we cannot readily reach by ourselves. For example: our back as well as specific methods to heal issues on both mental and emotional levels. These methods are explained in detail in the chapter on Absent Healing.

Q: *How long does it take to become a practitioner of Reiki?*

A: Generally, one becomes a Practitioner of Reiki after one has received the four attunements of Reiki First Degree. On the other hand, most people who wish to start a Reiki practice and wish to advertise themselves as a practitioner will often complete the practice requirements for the First Degree as well as the Second Degree workshop. For most, this process takes approximately 6 months or more. The emphasis is always on sound experience, a good understanding, as well as a personal integration of the methods learned.

CHAPTER EIGHT

'The purpose of life is not to be happy –
but to matter, to be productive, to be useful,
to have it make some difference that you lived at all.'

— LEO ROSTEN

Reiki Second degree

Reiki Second Degree is the next step of a traditional Western Reiki System.

Reiki II is a further increase of ones capacity to work with Universal energy and opens the door to increased personal empowerment. In Second Degree Reiki, participants receive the first three Reiki symbols. These are taught as a way to facilitate absent healing as well as various ways of working with Reiki energy.

In Reiki II there is also an increased empowerment with the Second Degree attunement.

The Result of the Second Degree Attunement

The prerequisite for receiving the Reiki II attunement requires the four First Degree Reiki attunements. Without these attunements, the energy and attunements will not work effectively. For example, if someone has completed Reiki First Degree with another teacher and wants to participate in a Reiki II workshop, they would need to be re-initiated into the particular Reiki lineage of the new teacher with the four Reiki I attunements. Without this, the Reiki II initiation will not work to its fullest capacity. The primary reason for this is that each attunement works in succession from each previous one. If one teacher's attunement procedure differs from that of another, then the bestowal of a new level loses its continuity, and therefore, the empowerment is incomplete.

As a result, the student will not be fully aligned with the particular lineage of the new initiating teacher. It is for this reason that the Reiki II initiation requires the previous attunements given in sequence for these to be activated within the student.

The Reiki II initiation expands on the pathway created by the four Reiki I attunements. In particular, this initiation gives the empowerment of the three Reiki II symbols.

This initiation doubles the capacity to channel Reiki energy, by expanding the channels of the Crown, Heart and Palm Chakras.

The Decision to Learn Second Degree

Before taking the next step in the Reiki system, one should consider one's motivation for advancing a level. One should also consider one's level of understanding and experience in the practices of Reiki First Degree. It is generally suggested that a student should actively use Reiki I for at least three months. Naturally, one may wish to do this sooner or later, but the suggested time frame is a good guideline to follow.

One can benefit from asking oneself the following questions:

1. How often do I give myself Reiki?
2. How many Reiki treatments have I given to others?
3. Do I remember and regularly practice the techniques of First Degree?
4. When was the last time I reviewed a Reiki First Degree workshop?
5. Do I feel ready to learn Second Degree?
6. Am I ready for greater self-empowerment?
7. Am I ready and willing to take responsibility to further my own healing?
8. Can I make time for further Reiki practice?
9. Have I asked for my Reiki teachers' opinion in this matter?

What is a Booster Attunement?

Although many Reiki styles do not utilize Booster Attunements, some styles do. These initiations hold the basic framework for the specific alignments of each level and act as a way to boost the practitioners' level of power and energy. The Booster attunements also act as a blessing, and a way to enjoy the experience that one receives from the attunement procedures. The Booster attunements are not an essential part of the empowerment procedures, and one does not need to be reliant on receiving Booster attunements as part of ones Reiki training. However, Booster attunements are very powerful and are a way to generate a large amount of spiritual power and energy in someone who receives them.

These attunements can be facilitated by practitioners who are not teachers of Reiki, provided they have completed and received the initiation for Reiki 3A. At this level the student can facilitate the Reiki level I Booster and the Reiki level II Booster attunements. The Reiki II Booster attunement should only be given to a Reiki practitioner who has completed and received the Reiki II initiation from a qualified Reiki instructor of the same lineage. The Reiki I Booster, on the other hand, can be given to anyone who wishes to experience the Reiki energy on a personal level. This particular attunement empowers an individual with the Reiki energy, however this alignment is only temporary. For a permanent result, one requires the four Reiki I attunements in sequence by a qualified teacher.

Reiki Symbology

The Reiki symbols act as pathways to the Reiki energy and enable the student to direct healing energy in specific ways.

In recent years, many teachers who have been taught in the Takata tradition have been sharing information on the symbols and their uses. In addition to this there has been an explosion of information published in books and in particular over the Internet. Much of this information details the Reiki symbols, their use as well as the attunement procedures.

One of the Reiki 'taboos' as taught by teachers of the old Western schools is the revealing of the Reiki symbols to the un-initiated student. What is often misunderstood is that without the actual empowerments for the Reiki symbols, their use has little or no effect. Without these empowerments from a qualified teacher of the lineage, using these symbols is like trying to drive a car without the keys – it simply won't work.

However, on the other hand, there is the sharing of information for practitioners who may or may not have accurate depictions of the Reiki symbols. In viewing these symbols the student can at least know what they have by comparison and thus correct their depictions, if need be.

In the old Western Reiki schools, it is still today a common practice that having viewed the Reiki symbols in the Second Degree workshop, one is required to commit these to memory. The symbols are then ritually burned at the end of the workshop. Unfortunately, this practice has for the most part resulted in a great deal of Reiki practitioners who are not able to remember the Reiki symbols.

In other cases, many students and teachers have completely inaccurate depictions of the original Reiki symbols, thus creating more confusion than sacredness. Fortunately, today many Reiki teachers have moved on from this practice and now supply their Reiki II students with visual representations of the Reiki symbols for personal reference.

The thing to know about symbols is that they do hold a matrix of power and energy. The other thing to know is that without the necessary empowerments the ability to tap this matrix of power and energy remains dormant. The way to awaken their power is via the Reiki attunements from a teacher who has this ability.

If you have an interest in viewing the Reiki symbols, a quick search on the Internet will satisfy your curiosity. A good search 'key word' combination is either: Reiki Symbols, Pictures of the Reiki Symbols, or Usui Reiki Symbols. Remember, without attunement into their use, they remain simply symbols.

The Union of Body, Speech and Mind

The Reiki symbols are in effect living energy fields. Each time a symbol is drawn by an initiated practitioner, the frequency of that symbol manifests. If we are to obtain the highest potential of each symbol, these symbols need to be drawn and pronounced precisely. In some Reiki schools, teachers advocate that it is the mantra that holds the symbols power, while in other schools a teacher may advocate that it is the symbol that holds the power. In actuality, the mantra and the symbols themselves are equal components. The union of these two elements creates a third energy, 'Mind' or 'Space'. This can be illustrated in the following way:

The physical depiction of a symbol represents the element of 'Body'. The Mantra (Japanese: kotodama) of each symbol represents the element of 'Speech'. These two parts combined create the third element of 'Mind'. Mind represents the energy of the symbol manifested. It is essential to summon both energies as this creates the third element or totality of the symbol's energy. For best results it is preferable to consciously sign and say the Reiki symbols with accuracy, in this way we create the form, sound and essence of each symbol into a living energy field.

Once a student has embodied these symbols on an inner level, these three elements come together without effort. The union of Body, Speech and Mind also represents the union of our own body, speech and mind. When we sign and say the symbols, we actually create a living field of energy that has an immediate energy effect on our own energy field.

It is when one signs these symbols without relying on memory or conscious effort that one has gone beyond concept and form. Once we have achieved this level, we open the door to realizing the true nature of the Reiki symbols.

Of course, all this may sound rather esoteric, but each symbol has a living energy which, when the properly attuned student prepares a solid foundation through regular practice, the realization of this becomes known. Each symbol in a way is a personality. Much in the same way one needs to spend time with someone to gain a good relationship, so it is with the Reiki symbols.

The Second Degree Reiki Symbols

In this following section we will describe some of the uses of the Reiki symbols as well as their names. Although some of the symbols uses will be described, the inner and secret practices are only reserved for the attuned student. The Japanese names for these mantras are called: 'Kotodama.' The mantras of each symbol are Japanese, yet their meaning in a modern Japanese dictionary is not necessarily literal. The origins of the Reiki symbols come from esoteric roots, and throughout time their inner meaning has remained secret only to the initiated student.

The following are the common descriptions and uses of the Reiki symbols given at Second Degree.

The first symbol is known as the 'Power symbol' and is generally spoken amongst the Reiki initiated under this name. The actual kotodama of the Power Symbol is: CHO KU REI. (pronounced: cho koo´ray).

The following are some of this symbol's uses:

- This symbol activates the Reiki energy. It draws 100% of the Reiki energy to one point fully focused.

- This symbol empowers all the other symbols and is usually used at the end of a sequence of symbols.

- Envisioned in three dimensions it may be used to draw energy from the energy field, and in the opposite fashion to draw energy into a point on the body.

- Choku Rei can be drawn over the hands before commencing a Reiki session. This is a way to active the Reiki energy immediately in the hands.

- The Choku Rei can be drawn over the entire body at the beginning and end of a treatment. Drawing it at the beginning opens the recipients' energy field to the healing energies. At the end, this symbol acts as a way to seal and protect the healing energy that has been transferred.

- The Choku Rei seals intention and can be used to empower affirmations.
- The Choku Rei magnifies and increases positive energy and decreases negative energy.

The second symbol taught in traditional Reiki is the symbol of 'Harmony'. The symbols kotodama is: SEI HE KI. (pronounced: say hay key). This symbol is also described as the mental, emotional healing symbol.

The following are some of the ways that this symbol is used:

- Sei Heki establishes Personal Boundaries, and acts as a filter for lower emotional and mental states.
- Sei Heki is a symbol for protection and can shield the practitioner from negativity.
- Sei Heki acts as a way to seal an individual from lower vibrational energy, psychic influences and negativity.
- Sei Heki activates the Divine Intelligence within. It activates the potential for the highest good within a situation or a person. It therefore creates order and harmony where there was disharmony.

The third symbol that is traditionally taught at Second Degree Reiki is the Symbol of 'Connection'. The Symbols kotodama is: HON SHA ZE SHO NEN, (pronounced: hon shar zay show nen) this symbol is also referred to as 'The Bridge'. This symbols main use is for Distant Healing, therefore the name: 'The Bridge' describes the movement of healing energy from one place or point in time to another.

The following are some of this symbols' uses in Reiki:

- The Honsha Ze Shonen is used to direct healing energy across time and space. It enables a bridging of energy and symbols from one place to another, regardless of time or distance. Energy can be sent whether it is past, present or projecting healing energy into the future. In effect this symbol acts as a time vehicle.
- Honsha Ze Shonen enables the practitioner to direct energy and symbols to more than one place at a time. It also bridges energy flow from one point of the body to another, especially where the hands are not in contact.
- This symbol is also used for balancing the Chakras.

- Honsha Ze Shonen is used for centering the mind in the present moment.
- This symbol is also used in absent healing to send healing energy and symbols to specific issues.

Signing the Second Degree Symbols

Learning the Reiki symbols includes committing them to memory. In Second Degree a practitioner should draw the symbols many times over, aiming for perfection with full awareness every time. Each time we sign a Reiki symbol we are signing the name of the sacred. It is a practice for training our minds and increasing focus.

If we take a lazy and unconscious approach to signing the Reiki symbols, we are affirming this in ourselves. Much like the Zen practice of signing one Japanese Kanji, thousands upon thousands of times to perfect the form, we aim for such dedication with the Reiki symbols. With time a deeper language begins to form and the wisdom of Reiki begins to penetrate our minds.

Non-Traditional Reiki Symbols

Non-traditional Reiki symbols are becoming more and more popular in Reiki classes worldwide. If a 'non-traditional' Reiki symbol is taught, it should be stated as being separate to the system. The reason for this is to keep the original system pure and to prevent confusion and wrong views. Unfortunately, many Reiki teachers do not make this distinction, and many students work with additional symbols rather than the ones described previously for Reiki II.

Perhaps with the attitude that 'More is Better', many additional non-Reiki items have been added to classes. As a result some Reiki workshops are more reminiscent of a diverse esoteric melting pot.

Mixing systems and styles creates confusion and defuses the effectiveness of a teaching. In an attempt to 'Jazz up' Reiki, the result is something other than the simplicity and purity of the original Reiki teachings.

Teaching symbols that differ from the four traditional Reiki symbols clearly indicates a deviation from the original Reiki system. This is not to say that other symbols do not hold power; however, it is paramount that a teacher giving a symbol be empowered to give it appropriately. This includes the correct empowerment and permission necessary to make this alignment in the student.

With this in mind a student should seek to know which symbols will be taught by their chosen teacher. It is important to know that the symbols have a lineage and that the teacher concerned is empowered to pass these on appropriately.

Modes of Perception

The symbols of traditional Reiki offer a Second Degree student a number of new resources for healing. At the Reiki II level we can utilize the symbols to do the following:

1. To establish our personal boundaries.
2. To activate the flow of Reiki energy.
3. To clear blockages or lower energetic patterns.
4. To balance the energy centers (Chakras).
5. For accessing information from a variety of means on visual, auditory and kinesthetic levels.
6. To send Absent Healing.
7. To increase Reiki energy.
8. To activate healing outcomes to numerous situations.
9. To clear lower energy from our environments.
10. To establish protection and for sealing healing energy.

Tuning Ones' Perception

When healing others with Reiki, there are many ways to utilize the senses to gain information for directing healing energy. The most common ways we perceive impressions from the outer and inner world is through our Visual, Kinesthetic and Auditory modes of perception. By daily use of any of these modes we experience the world. When we see a person by utilizing our visual mode, we experience their image visually. This may elicit an emotion or feeling and here we utilize our Kinesthetic more. For example, we may feel an attraction or an aversion to the person. With our auditory mode, our internal dialogue may be along the lines of " I'd love to spend some time with this person", or "I don't like that person". So, in a few moments we may have operated on a visual level (seeing the person and using our imagination); on a kinesthetic level (feeling drawn or repelled to the person), and lastly on an auditory level (the internal dialogue associated with our response to the person).

Our modes of perception operate constantly and mostly without our conscious awareness of their presence. Intuitively, our modes of perception are very useful in healing work and can be used to greatly assist with the ability to sense areas of imbalance during our sessions. These methods can also be used in our daily lives with regard to accessing information, decision-making and generally living more intuitively.

By using our perception as a tool to access information, we are simply slowing down our usual processes. By asking the right kind of questions and getting to know how our intuition operates, we have a method for accessing information on a conscious level. Everyone has this ability and it can be learned. All we need to do is know how to hone these skills for healing.

Accessing our Current State

Also described as 'checking in', this method can be used as a preliminary procedure before we begin a Reiki treatment. This technique is also a way to monitor or access information that bypasses our physical minds. In this way we can go directly to our Higher or Transpersonal Self.

In a way it is much like using an internal pendulum. We can learn how to access a 'yes' or 'no' response.

Procedure:

Place your hands on your upper chest and ask yourself a simple question, for example: "Am I energetically clear to commence this healing session?"

Upon asking this question, there is always an immediate response. This occurs through one of our modes of perception, primarily: Visual, Auditory or Kinesthetic.

The following are examples that may indicate a 'Yes' response.

Visual	- seeing or sensing a bright color or a positive image.
Kinesthetic	- a rising feeling in the body or head. Or an engaging and embracing feeling.
Auditory	- the word in our mind 'Yes' or some other dialogue to this effect.

A 'No' response might be:

Visual	- Seeing or sensing a dull color or experiencing a negative image.
Kinesthetic	- A sinking feeling in the lower belly or a pushing back, or pulling away feeling.
Auditory	- The word 'No' or words to this effect.

These are common examples, yet they are not exclusive in their interpretation. By working with awareness and perception, a pattern for receiving information tends to unfold which is unique for each person. As this evolves, we can learn to perceive a pattern of how our modes commonly operate.

A helpful hint when using this method is to always go with your first impression. When asking a question, in this way, the response is almost always immediate. Many of us are taught from an early age not to trust our intuitive responses, and to look for a logical and cognitive understanding. So when someone asks themselves a question, the first obstacle they encounter is their Ego mind. This takes the form of Doubt, Judgment and Fear. We doubt we are correct, we then Judge our impression and Fear others will judge our experience. The simple solution to this is to trust your first intuitive response or impression. This will always lead you to a true and correct answer to your question.

This same procedure can be applied to just about any decision or choice to be made. Using this technique, we bypass our physical mind and go directly to our intuition. Another extension of this is to hold an object with awareness. For example: You may want to purchase a book. Hold the book in your hands and tune in. Ask the question: "Is this an appropriate book for me?" and wait for your immediate response or impression. Try it and see for yourself! This is your intuition talking.

Another excellent way to access your intuitive responses is using the Bai Hui point, which is situated on the crown of your head. To find this exact point, one draws a line from the bottom of the lobe to the top of the ear, and follows this angle up to the top of the head. Another way to find this point is to place your own hands on your head and measure, eight finger widths from your original hairline, back to the center of your head. If you do this correctly, both approaches will lead you to the same spot.

This point is a major point of energy flow and is a direct way to gain an intuitive response. In the same situation as illustrated before, one could place an object on their Bai Hui point and tune in for a response on a visual, kinesthetic or auditory level.

Negative Transference

A common concern in healing is that we will experience our clients' symptoms transferring into our body. Although this experience is not common, transference can occur in a variety of ways either physically, emotionally, psychically and/or spiritually. Often the reason for this occurring is due to the practitioner neglecting to establish his or her own personal boundaries.

Creating a personal boundary is usually done before commencing a Reiki treatment. It is important to have an awareness of boundaries whenever an energetic exchange occurs. The benefit of working with the Reiki energy is that the very nature of Reiki has a strong protective quality. This protection is imparted during the attunement procedures. As a result, whenever we facilitate healing for another, this protective quality of Reiki is always there. Although we are in a protected energy field, we can enhance our boundaries by engaging in the 'Protection and Boundaries' procedure. Creating an energetic boundary adds a 'safety net' to healing work. When we look at most traditional forms of hands on healing, whether it is from indigenous healing traditions or Western mysticism, there is always some preliminary procedure for personal boundaries that a practitioner follows. Whether this involves calling in one's allies through prayer, visualization, invocation or a myriad range of techniques, a sense of 'self' during healing defines the boundaries and assists in maintaining a sound protection. Therefore, it makes sense to apply this fundamental law to our healing work. Creating a boundary becomes more emphasized when we are dealing with very ill or negative people. When we establish our intent for healing and set up the appropriate conditions, we greatly enhance our personal and spiritual strength.

Establishing Personal Boundaries

This is an invaluable practice for anyone in health care professions, i.e., nursing, hospice, mental health, or in general for times when we feel that we are taking on unnecessary emotional or mental energy from another.

There are certain situations in life and when healing the ill that call for additional protection. The Sei Heki symbol when used for protection is a direct way to boost our psychic defenses. Many of us have experienced being in the presence of someone who is depressed or sad. After a period of being exposed to their energy, it starts to rub off on us and we begin to feel heavy or down ourselves. This is a classic example of lower energy transference.

A regular comment from remedial massage therapists is that they often experience pain in their hands in relation to a tension spot on their client, or experience the feeling of being drained after a session.

Another example is when someone is conducting a session and experiences the clients' symptoms in his or her own body. This is referred to as "telesomatic transference".

Some native healers use this method for diagnosing and removing harmful influences in their clients. However they are specialists in these kinds of methods and often have preliminarily processes which they engage in to deal with these harmful energies.

In the Reiki system, there are ways to establish the appropriate boundaries. As a precaution to transference occurring, we use the protective quality of the Sei Heki. The following is a procedure for activating your personal boundaries with the second Reiki II symbol, the Sei Heki.

Procedure:

Sign the Sei Heki symbol over your palms. Imagine that the symbol is imbedded in your palms in a blue light.*

Blue light represents all the healing energies of the Reiki system and the color corresponds to the vibration of protection.

Now place your hands on your upper chest. As soon as your hands make contact with your body, imagine a blue sphere manifests inside your chest and inside the sphere is the Sei Heki symbol radiating blue light. Now in the same way you would blow up a balloon, with each exhale the sphere in your chest expands more and more. Keep exhaling and expanding the sphere until your entire body is enveloped in this radiant energy field of protection. Once you feel that your body is completely surrounded by this energy field, imagine that a large Sei Heki is wrapped around your body like a cape. This effectively creates a protective energy field and with practice one becomes more effective in creating this energy field. For Reiki First Degree students who do not have the attunement for the Second Degree symbols, the same exercise can be performed without the symbol by just using the blue energy field.

This exercise can also be extended into daily life. When we are in a public place, for example a hospital, it is not always possible to drop everything and place our hands on our body and begin the meditation, especially if we have an on-looking audience. So this can be facilitated as a visualization or mental intention. We can quickly imagine the Sei Heki wrapped around us with one part of the symbol on either side of our body in the color blue, much like wearing a protective coat around you. Alternatively one can see themselves in a blue energy field that wards off unwanted energy.

Clearing Energy

There are times when we do take on the process of another in the form of transference. This is usually when we have had a negative interaction with another, in the form of an argument, conversation or simply by being around a negative person or in a negative environment. When this does occur, we can clear this lower vibration energy from ourselves by passing the Sei Heki symbol through our energy field, thereby raising the body's frequency. When we do this, the higher vibration of the Reiki symbol transmutes the lower frequency. We can also clear ourselves when we are feeling sluggish or when our own vibration is low. Remember, the Reiki symbols are living energy fields. Each time a symbol is drawn, the field effect occurs. Effectively we raise our vibration and thus strengthen our energy field.

The procedure is as follows:

Visualize or draw a large Sei Heki in front of you, seeing it in the color blue. The symbol should be the same size as you, and directly in front. Now in your mind's eye, pass this symbol through your energy field and body, back and forth three times.

When we do this exercise, we raise our vibration and resonance to a higher frequency and the lower vibration energy is transmuted to this level. To expand on this, we can also affirm in our minds the following: "I now clear any lesser or lower energies, these energies now leave this vessel and all lower energy is now transformed into the highest good."

This whole process may be repeated three times or until you feel clear.

Other Methods of Cleansing

Some other ways to cleanse your energy field is to burn native herbs and use the smoke to cleanse or 'smudge' your energy field. 'Smudging' is an ancient practice of using particular herbs to ceremonially cleanse the body and energy field of negative influences and feelings. These herbs have a direct effect and promote energetic clarity.

• Herbs that are commonly used for cleansing are sage, cedar, sweet grass and sandalwood.

• Smudge sticks are widely available in most New-Age stores.

Salt water

Salt water is another excellent gift from nature that cleanses the human energy field almost immediately. A swim in the ocean for 5 to 10 minutes will clear any lower energy from your field and restore balance to your vital energy. If the ocean is not accessible, a salt bath is another good alternative.

Place two generous handfuls of rock salt or sea salt into a bath, and raise the water to a comfortable depth and temperature. Soak for 15 minutes and allow the salt to melt away any lower vibration energy.

Cleansing Breaths Procedure

When you are just about ready to get out of the bath, release the water and focus on your 'out breaths'. As you are breathing out, visualize that any remaining discursive thoughts, feelings or energy is leaving your body with the water. Imagine this energy is leaving via the palms of your hands and the soles of your feet. You will generally feel relaxed but a little drained from this process.

Follow the bath with a clean water shower and imagine the water is not only running over your body but through it, clearing any lower energies as it does. Once finished lay down and apply the Reiki self-healing procedure for about 15 minutes. This will revitalize your energy field.

During the self-healing, focus on your 'in breath', imagine with each breath that you are drawing in vital energy from your palms and see it disperse throughout your body. This will also enhance the re-energizing process.

The process of releasing the breath can be used anytime to center and remove unwanted energy. If you are standing or seated, imagine the breath leaving via the soles of the feet and going into the earth, where the natural forces of nature can transmute this energy.

Cleansing Rooms or a Location with the Reiki Symbols

It makes sense to do a spring clean every now and then, but how often do we consider our energetic environment? Have you ever entered a room and received the feeling like you wanted to leave because it didn't feel right? This is often the result of lower vibrational energy within a room.

There is a simple procedure to clear these lower vibrations and to call in a higher frequency.

If you operate your Reiki treatments out of a room on a regular basis, then this practice can be a regular event and will enhance your personal environment.

Places of illness and death are lower vibration energy havens. Such as: Funeral directors, hospitals, veterinary clinics, etc. This procedure can also be sent as an absent healing procedure.

Clearing Rooms Procedure

First of all, open a window or door. This allows the old energy to disperse.

1. Begin at the center of the room. Fold your hands at your heart and take a few moments to still your mind.

2. We now center ourselves, and seal our personal boundaries as described previously. Once we feel centered, we go to a corner of the room. With one hand on our heart and the other hand extended in front of us, we sign a large Choku Rei symbol in the air. This can be drawn with our hand or we can incorporate a smudge stick or incense stick into the procedure by signing the symbol with the stick.

3. Now we walk to the next corner and while we are walking, we affirm either silently or aloud, "I now clear any lesser or lower energies from this room, all is transformed into the highest good."

4. Having arrived at the next corner, we then sign another large Choku Rei and repeat the affirmation to the next corner and so on, until we have reached the corner where we started.

Bringing Healing Energy into a Room

This procedure follows the clearing procedure. Having cleared the room, we can now bring in a positive influence.

1. Stand at the center of the room and face east.

   Holding your hand in front of you, sign a large Choku Rei to that direction, stating the name of the symbol three times. Now bring your hand to your heart center and cup the symbol here also.

2. Face north and sign the symbol again, bringing your cupped hand at the heart.

   Now you have two cupped symbols at your heart.

3. Face west and repeat the process, one to the west, one cupped at your heart.

4. Repeat the same for the south.

5. Face east again (you should now have four symbols cupped in your hand).

   Draw Choku Rei again over your cupped hand, followed by: Honsha Ze Shonen, Sei Heki and again with the Choku Rei.

6. Give a prayer of intent. State: "I now call forth all the highest healing energies into this room. May whatever merit that is generated through this practice benefit all that lives".

7. Now as if you have a ball in your hands, throw this energy up into the sky.

   Leave your hands out to the sides. One will often feel the energy raining down over ones head and into the room.

This exercise will call the Reiki energy into the room. You may wish to use one of the other symbols for each direction or a symbol stack. Determine which symbol feels appropriate for each situation.

If we follow the Universal law that love and fear cannot occupy the same space, when we establish the Reiki energy in a room on a regular basis, we build up the higher frequency of love. This also has a protective quality. It is like a type of 'spiritual teflon coating'; negativity just slides off and can't penetrate the positive energy field.

These procedures also work especially well in absent healing. I know of a teacher who sent absent healing to his classroom each morning and was astounded by the way his students behaved. He also noticed that when he missed a day, his students misbehaved.

Purification

We can actively cleanse our minds of negative energy patterns by utilizing the following method for focusing. This aids in removing obstacles to our path and healing.

The procedure is as follows:

1. Sit or lie in a room, close your eyes and bring to mind a particular problem, emotion, illness, etc. Think about this and make this issue strong in your mind.
2. Now, focusing on this issue, ask yourself the question: 'If this issue resided in my body, where would it reside?' Now tune into your body and locate the area where this issue resides.
3. Place your hands on this area and give yourself Reiki.
4. Now think to yourself- 'If this issue had a form, sensation or color what would it be?' Imagine this issue in a particular form, color or sensation.
5. Once you have an impression of the issues form or sensation, imagine a brilliant white light penetrating this issue. Imagine this light reducing the problem in size, dissolving or extracting this from your body. Keep imagining this until there is no remnant of this issue.
6. Once this issue has been removed and purified, imagine a sphere or some symbol that holds power and spiritual meaning for you. See the symbol in this place, radiating light, healing and protection. This can be imagined throughout the day or as needed.

Accumulating Power and Protection

Once you have cleansed yourself you can develop power and protection in the following manner.

The procedure is as follows:

1. Imagine yourself sitting in a circle and that you are at the center of the circle. You also may wish to actually draw a physical circle around you as you visualize this process.

2. Now imagine that there are numerous duplicates of yourself surrounding you at the perimeter of the circle. These duplicates of your self are beautiful, powerful and filled with energy and protection. Take time to build these images of yourself. Once you feel happy with the images of yourself looking youthful, spiritually strong and positive, filled with healing power, see these expressions of yourself moving one by one towards you.

3. As each one merges with your body, feel yourself filling with their power, protection and healing energies. You are becoming their power and filling more and more with their light and healing.

4. Continue this until all the emanations of yourself have filled your body. You are now filled with their positive energy, spiritual power and protection.

You may wish to vary this by imagining various Buddha's around you, a Spiritual friend or teacher, Reiki symbols or some other symbol that holds spiritual meaning for you. The more one does this, the greater power one generates. One should understand that these practices are not designed so that you can become some kind of powerful magician. When we have more energy and power, we can do more for others in a compassionate way. We have a greater capacity to be kind and have the energy to do more beneficial activities.

'One who thinks and acts to achieve his own ends is a worldly being. One who thinks and works for others' welfare alone is a Dharma practitioner.'

— JAMGON KONGTRUL, MIND TRAINING IN SEVEN POINTS

Hands-on Healing for Second Degree

Having explored a number of preliminary procedures, here is the condensed procedure for facilitating a Reiki treatment. The methods presented here include and extend beyond the checklist for a level one practitioner and also utilize the Reiki symbols.

1. Gather information from the recipient regarding their needs.

    Ask: Have you had a Reiki Session before? If not, briefly explain the process.*

    *Here one will state that Reiki is the transference of Universal Healing Energy and that you will be placing your hands on the areas of imbalance to restore the vital energy within their being.

    Ask: Is there anywhere that you require healing?

    Once you have a general idea of what they require, ask them to close their eyes and relax. It is usually recommended that both you and the client keep the talking to a bare minimum, so that they can receive the maximum benefit from the treatment and so that you can concentrate on what you are doing. It is important to check whether they are comfortable and to ask whether your hands are too light or too heavy. One should never introduce movement with hands on healing and the hands should always rest gently on the persons' body.

2. *Centering Procedure*: Place your hands on your upper chest and close your eyes.

    Focus your intent for a brief moment. Imagine yourself being a

vessel for the Universal energy and that you are being completely filled from your feet to the top of your head with healing
energies. This can be imaged as a white light pouring from the
Universal source above the top of your head. One can also imagine that from the source above you a large Choku Rei is spiraling
down and through your energy field, purifying and centering
you.

3. *Clearing*: This next exercise can be done if you feel a need to clear
   your energy field. Visualize the Sei Heki in front of you. Now
   imagine this symbol in the color blue and pass it through your
   body and energy field, purifying any areas of imbalance. Affirm
   in your mind as this is occurring: 'I now clear any lesser and
   lower energy from my body and mind, and only the highest energies remain. All is transformed into the healing power of
   Reiki.'

   Repeat this process three times, projecting the symbol back and
   forth through your energy field or until you feel clear.

4. *Personal Boundaries:* Now seal your energy field with a blue Sei
   Heki, stating the name of the symbol three times. This establishes your personal boundaries throughout the healing procedure.

5. *Treatment:* Begin by signing a large Choku Rei over the recipients' body. This opens their energy field to the Reiki energy.
   Now in your own way commence the session. Employ scanning
   techniques and internal dialogue.

   Ask inwardly:
   • 'Where would you like my hands?'
   • 'Do you require any symbols?'
   • 'Have you had enough energy?'
   • 'Where would you like my hands next?'

6. Once you feel the healing is complete, sign a large Choku Rei
   over their body, this seals in the healing. Now imagine that there
   is a blue energy field much like a bubble in your mouth. Blow
   this through your hands and sense that any lower energy is dispelled instantaneously. This also disconnects you from the
   recipient's energy field.

7. Wash your hands, then gently bring the person around and share
   your experiences. Be sure not to interpret or diagnose their condition. Simply share what you sensed during the treatment.

Second Degree Hands on Healing Techniques

In addition to the procedures outlined previously, there are a number of ways to apply Reiki healing for oneself or another. Essentially there are two approaches. The first being a sequential step by step approach and the other being an intuitive approach. Intuitive healing is comprised of eight major avenues. We will explore these methods here, but first a brief outline of the traditional hands on healing sequence, which includes the Reiki symbols.

1. Traditional Hand Positions

    Following the sequence of the hand positions from First Degree Reiki, we can visualize or draw the Choku Rei where our hands are in contact to magnify the healing energy flowing through to the participant. This same procedure is followed for each new hand position. One signs a Choku Rei just prior to placing the hands on the area of the body. Then one places their hands on the person and visualizes the symbol merging into the place where the hands are in contact.

2. Intuitive Healing

    Here, we depart from a step-by-step approach and utilize a variety of ways to direct healing intuitively.

    These methods use various modes of perception to obtain information regarding the individuals healing. These methods include both psychic and clairvoyant approaches and employ scanning, seeing, beaming, clearing and extracting, transmuting, infusing, smoothing, raking, and internal dialogue techniques.

    So let's map these out one by one.

    A. Scanning

    This technique falls under the kinesthetic mode of perception. Here we use our hands to scan the energy field just above the body, (generally 2-3 inches from the body). This is usually conducted at the beginning of a session, and is facilitated from the top of the body to the bottom. The practitioner may repeat this process a number of times throughout the session or in parts, depending upon the individual case.

    As we scan, what are we looking for? The sensations that can be experienced are varied and may include a feeling of warmth or tingling in the palms, heaviness, or a strong feeling that the hands want to be placed in an area. All these sensations generally indicate a place that requires healing.

B. Seeing

This technique uses the eyes, and falls under the category of a visual mode of perception.

Here, we look down the body in a way similar to scanning. In this approach we are looking into the body and energy field. Not everyone sees auras, and in most cases we sense rather than see areas that require healing. As we look down and through the body, we may sense dull or vibrant areas in the energy field and body. Generally dull colors indicate congestion, depletion and imbalance, whereas the vibrant colors indicate health and vitality. As part of this procedure, we imagine that we are viewing the internal organs of the body. It is almost like we are viewing each organ as if they were translucent. While using this technique, we look for or sense dull or heavy areas. Once we have identified the depleted or diseased areas, we can begin the process of clearing these with symbols, creative visualization and Reiki energy.

C. Beaming

In this method we project healing energy from our palms to the recipient. Here the hands are held off the body. We may even be some distance from the person and with our intent we direct healing energy and symbols to the person and afflicted areas. This approach can also be utilized using the eyes, directing healing energy and symbols from our eyes to the affected area. One can also direct healing energy from our heart Chakra to the person requiring healing. Directing healing energy from the heart is particularly useful with issues concerning the giving and receiving of love, intimacy issues and for creating feelings of safety.

D. Clearing and Extracting

In this procedure the practitioner is removing harmful energies from the individual. These can be extracted using the Choku Rei in a reverse fashion, spiraling outwards, anticlockwise, and pulling the negative energy with it. This lower energy can then be transmuted, as described in the next technique. A practitioner may also remove these obstacles with both hands, as if pulling out a physical object. This can also be visualized whilst the hands are within the energy field. Another method of extracting and clearing energy is sucking the diseased energy via the mouth. This is a practice common among many indigenous healers; however, this procedure is also very dangerous. With this method, the practitioner is highly susceptible to receiving this lower vibration energy, and can be greatly affected if they do not have the skill to deal with these energies once they are inside their body. Even among highly skilled native healers, the result of such methods often has a debilitating effect on the Shaman. Many healers who utilize this method can for days or in some cases even weeks, feel the repercussions of these energies. As a general rule of thumb, it is not recommended to use this particular method, as the risks are simply too high. Other methods of extracting can safely be used with a quartz crystal, where the lower energy is drawn into the crystal, to later be cleansed and transmuted.

A healer may also visualize the lower energy leaving the body via the openings of the body, hands or soles of the feet as black smoke, creepy crawlies or black sludge. These should be seen as leaving the body and going deep into the earth, or transmuted into positive symbols or healing energy.

E. Transmuting

In this approach, once negative energy has been extracted from the energy field, the practitioner can transmute this energy into a positive energy or simply release it. This is done using the Sei Heki. Once the energy is drawn out using the Choku Rei, it is kept in the hand and the practitioner blows or infuses a Sei Heki, into their hand, which transmutes this into positive energy. Practitioners also may visualize the harmful energy transmuting into light, diamonds, stars and the like and then proceed to place these back into the body, via the method of infusing. Lower vibration energy can also be transmuted using a bucket of salty water. Once the negative energy is removed from the body and energy field, it is thrown or projected into the salt water. This is a common practice utilized by Pranic Healers. The water absorbs the negative energy and the salt breaks down the negative energies and makes them neutral. Ideally, a Reiki practitioner will use symbols for transmuting energy directly and this is the preferred method.

In some healing circles, you will occasionally see a healer throw negative energy behind them on the floor, or shaking their hands as if trying to flick off something. This is an inappropriate practice, as it is a form of psychic littering. If lower vibration energy is thrown away, without the conscious intent to transmute it, it will simply hang around and transfer onto some other unsuspecting person, or even the person it was extracted from in the first place when they get off the table after the session. This is why it is very important to transmute energy, and the more the better as it is turned into something positive.

F. Infusing

Infusing uses the breath to implant symbols into the body. Infusing can also clear meridians, Chakras or the central energy channel which runs through the center of the body. This is propelled with a short sharp breath from the belly. The intent is to infuse a symbol into the area that requires healing. The practitioner may also use this method for transmuting negative energy that has been extracted, and change it into a positive energy, by infusing the Sei Heki symbol.

G. Smoothing and Raking the Aura

Smoothing the Aura at the end of a session is a way to balance the field from the activity that has taken place during the healing. This is done with both hands, fingers spread, from the crown Chakra to the feet, usually three consecutive times. The hands should be approximately 2 to 3 inches from the body.

Raking the aura is a way to energize and ground the recipient after a healing. This is the same procedure as smoothing, but instead the practitioner starts at the feet and makes their way to the crown and the hands have the fingers spread wide open, much like a rake. Usually, 'Raking' is followed by 'Smoothing' at the end of a healing treatment. These same methods can also be applied when the person is seated. After the treatment, smooth the Aura from the back of the head to the base of the spine. Repeat this procedure in a reverse fashion, from the base to the crown with the raking technique.

H. Internal dialogue

This technique enables a conversation using simple 'Yes/No' responses and the naming of body areas to direct healing energy. We begin by asking the question: 'What does this person require to be healed?'

The following is a hypothetical internal dialogue one might encounter during a healing session.

F = Facilitator of the healing

RTPS = Recipient's Transpersonal Self

For example:

F: 'Where would you like my hands?' RTPS: 'Upper chest and forehead.'

F: 'Do you require any symbols here?' RTPS: 'Choku Rei and Sei Heki.'

F: 'Have you had enough energy here?' RTPS: 'Yes.'

F: 'Where else would you like my hands next?' RTPS: 'Shoulders, etc...'

As we become more adept at these processes, we usually find that there may be a number of the previously mentioned modes of perception interchanging or working simultaneously. It should be pointed out that one does not simply have all of these abilities as a beginner of Reiki. Be patient when trying these approaches, they will develop in time as you grow with Reiki.

'Like an enemy waiting in ambush,
disease comes without warning.'

— SANGWA TULKU

Absent Healing

Absent healing is one of the primary methods taught in Second Degree Reiki. Here we move beyond the physical level and boldly venture into new and exciting dimensions.

With Absent Healing we have the ability to send healing to present situations, events and people as well as ourselves. We can also direct healing energy to past situations to affect our current outlook, and into the future to set up favorable circumstances for our lives.

So how does Absent Healing work? Using the Reiki symbols as a gateway for universal energy, we use the spiritual law of correspondence to direct energy to whichever time and space we desire.

The symbol that is the primary tool for this is the Honsha Ze Shonen. In a way one could look at this symbol as a time vehicle. With this symbol, one can send healing to someone on the other side of the world and they will experience the result, as if you were physically present with them. There are no time delays, it happens in that moment, regardless of time zones in different countries.

The Quantum Universe

The Webster's Dictionary describes Quantum as: 'a theory in physics based on the concept of subdivision of radiant energy into finite quanta and applied to numerous processes involving transference or transformation of energy in an atomic or molecular scale.' In layman's terms, this means we are all interconnected.

We live in a quantum universe. What this means is that on the subatomic level, these tiny particles (which make up the very fabric of the universe) are interconnected and unified and this unified field has intelligence. For example, a subatomic particle will know what another subatomic particle knows on the other side of the world, or the other side of the galaxy for that matter. There are no time delays involved, and it is not a question of faster than the speed of light because it occurs instantly.

What Quantum theory suggests is that there is interconnectedness between all life and that anywhere on the scale between the macrocosm and microcosm, intelligence is present.

In the spiritual order of things this is nothing new, for the mystics of old have utilized these laws for centuries. These same laws govern Absent Healing.

Absent Healing utilizes symbols as a pathway on which the Reiki energy can travel. We actively shape this intelligent energy from one place, time or space to another. This occurs at the same time, creating the desired result, which is the transference of healing energy.

With Absent Healing we can begin to shape our reality and to determine the outcome of events that will benefit all, by shaping Universal Intelligence and using the power of our minds. This shaping is a union between our own mind, the mind of the person involved and the Universal Energy, or higher intelligence or if you like *Star Wars*, 'The Force'.

The analogy of 'The Force' as portrayed in the *Star Wars* Trilogy is a beautiful example to demonstrate Universal Energy. It suggests that the Universe has a force and this force is neutral. Then it is channeled in either light or dark ways. There is the good side of the Force, and the dark side of the Force, yet it is still the Force, simply being shaped by the practitioner. What determines the kind of force comes down to one's intent and personal motivation.

To work with the dark side, one simply operates out of ignorance and is driven by emotions like greed, manipulation, power, self-delusion, egotism and the desire to harm. To work out of the good side is to operate out of love, compassion, unity, peace, joy, healing and happiness. Essentially there is a fine line between healing and sorcery. Our vehicle is our motivation, or intention, whether they are life giving or life destroying. Other methods of healing work, which have a basis in dualistic sources, can operate in either light or dark ways depending upon the practitioner. Fortunately with Reiki it is very hard to utilize this energy in a harmful way as a practitioner is united with a Universal field that operates out of love and compassion for all beings.

The Universal Law of Correspondence

The Law of Correspondence works on the premise that if we use an object, effigy or proxy as a point of focus for the healing energy we wish to transfer, then the object will be the means to create a link to the person we wish to heal.

A common example of how an effigy is used that many can relate to, is the use of the Voodoo Doll. Perhaps this is not the best example in light of the fact that we are talking about healing, but in a sense, there is little difference in healing and sorcery, as intent plays a big part. Using a Voodoo Doll to represent a person to be harmed, the Voodoo practitioner administers pain to the doll, along with malice intentions to transfer harm to the person. In Absent Healing we can also utilize an object to represent a person, such as a teddy bear. We then correspond healing energy to the person, via hands on healing to the object and by creating a link to the person via the Reiki symbols. All these factors create the right ingredients for a beneficial effect. The difference is the intention for healing instead of harm and even more importantly we are drawing our healing energy from a benevolent and intelligent source of energy.

This spiritual law is the basis for almost all non-local healing work. In using the Reiki symbols to form a bridge, we can effectively make a pathway for the Reiki energy to travel. This process transcends ordinary time, as it is not fixed in three dimensional time and space. The Reiki symbols go beyond the physical level and as a result are not bound by the laws of linear time. Not only can a practitioner send a distant healing to a person's injury in another country, one can also send healing energy to the cause of the injury which may have occurred months or even years ago and will effect the current situation in a beneficial way.

How to Send an Absent Healing

The following is one of the procedures given to Reiki II students.

Where possible, gain conscious permission from the recipient.

You will need the name and location of the person. You will need a proxy (i.e., a teddy bear) and/or a photograph of the person.

1. Center your self and establish boundaries as in the checklist for hands on healing.

2. Calling in and establishing permission:

   Hold both hands out in front of you and declare: 'Sei Heki, Sei Heki, Sei Heki. Name, Name, Name (person concerned) Are you there?' At this point you will get a sense of the thought form of the individual, between your hands.

State: 'Are you free to accept this healing at an appropriate time for you?'

If you receive a firm 'Yes', proceed.

If you receive a firm 'No', blow through your hands three times and dismiss.

Once you have a 'Yes' to the healing, STATE : At which time the healing will transfer, or if unknown: 'This healing energy transfers now or from the time that you go to sleep, to the time you wake up'.

3. With hands still cupped, with one hand, draw over the other:

   HONSHA ZE SHONEN. This creates a bridge to the person's energy field.

   SEI HEKI. This creates the energy for harmony.

   CHOKU REI. This creates a pathway of Universal Energy and opens the energy.

4. Now transfer your cupped hands gently to the proxy.

   You are now sending healing energy, (or at the time stated), to the recipient.

5. While you are sending the energy, be open to receiving information concerning their healing.

   Ask: 'Is there anywhere you would like my hands?'

   'Do you require any symbols?', etc.

6. Send for as long as is needed, implement scanning and clearing procedures, if required.

7. Once the healing is complete, slowly move your hands from the proxy, and once again cup your hands in front of you.

   Draw:

   CHOKU REI (This seals the healing.)

8. Bless and dismiss. State: 'You are now dismissed, may you be well and happy.'

   Blow through cupped hands three times. This releases the persons' thought form.

Methods for Absent Healing

If we look at the various ways to send an absent healing, there are essentially four methods. The following techniques can be implemented after the individual has been 'called in' with the three symbols and the bridge has been drawn to the recipient.

Method 1: Using your body as a proxy

Here we use the law of correspondence, utilizing both our knees and thighs as our proxy.

In this approach we identify our right knee to correspond to the head of the recipient. Then working our way down our thigh, stating: "My upper thigh now corresponds to the recipient's upper chest", with the opposite knee and thigh corresponding to the back of the head and the upper thigh corresponding to the recipient's shoulders and upper back. It is like the person is split in two down the length of their body so each side is facing you as you look at your thighs. This method is best to do while seated.

A further extension of this is to give yourself a Reiki treatment, with the hand positions and your body corresponding to the person you are sending to. In this way you are facilitating a Reiki self-treatment, as well as sending absent healing to another. You are effectively in two places at once. If you choose to do this method it is best to only give this method of Absent Healing to someone who you would feel comfortable giving a hug. As we are inviting the persons' energy field into our own body, it is in our best energetic interest not to open our energies to transference. This is particularly important in the case where the person concerned is chronically ill, mentally disturbed or emotionally unstable. In situations like these it is better to use a proxy as it gives some distance from their condition and your own energy system.

Method 2: Using a teddy bear as a proxy

With this method, instead of using your body as a proxy, we use a teddy bear to represent the individual receiving the healing. This method is a good extension when facilitating absent healing on the inner child or issues from the past.

Another extension is to use a pillow or pillows on a massage table, much like a mannequin, and to commence a full treatment as if the person was lying on the massage table.

Anything can be used as a proxy, i.e., a handbag, a rolled up sweater, a crystal, etc. Using the law of correspondence, we can apply this method to anything as a proxy. The only thing to remember is to follow the method for Absent Healing previously mentioned.

Method 3: Cupped hands

Here we use the space between our cupped hands and visualize
that our hands are now holding a certain area of the body, or the
whole person for the matter. This technique works particularly
well for healing issues or for manifesting goals. In addition to this,
we can also use this method as a way to work on the inner organs
of the body. For example: "My hands are now holding the spleen of
the recipient."

Method 4: Visualization

In this method we simply visualize ourselves healing the individual. We visualize that we are present with them and that they
are receiving hands-on healing from ourselves. This technique requires greater mental focus, so it is suggested not to have any outside distractions where possible.

Sending Healing Energy to a Situation

Sending Reiki to a situation that requires resolve or healing is another way to work with absent healing. This process uses the same
procedure, as before, the only difference is the 'calling in' stage. In
this stage we state the situation clearly and precisely three times
until we feel contact with the issue between our hands. Then we
follow the usual procedure as in the checklist for Absent Healing.
For example: I am now calling: 'The healing resolve between my
father and myself. The healing resolve between my father and
myself', etc., stating the intent three times.

Sending Healing to More than One Person

Group healing is a way to be more effective in your healing practice because you can effectively be in more than one place at once.
    What this requires is an individual 'calling in' procedure, and
the signing of the three symbols which creates a bridge to not only
one individual, but to several.

The procedure is as follows:

After establishing boundaries and setting your intent for healing,
call in each person by name and location, and sign the three symbols on each person. This can be in the form of an individual photograph or an individual piece of paper with the person's details
on it. Once you have called in all the individuals concerned, move
your hands to a proxy of your choice, stating that this proxy corresponds to all the individuals in the photographs. Send for approximately 10 to 20 minutes and close with the Choku Rei, and blow
through your cupped hands.

Essentially, each individual called in has received the required amount of energy. When directing the healing, it is best to utilize the complete sequence of hand positions, as this way you'll cover all areas required in the treatment of all concerned.

A common misconception that one may assume from this procedure is, "If the Reiki energy is infinite, why can't I just send an Absent Healing to one hundred people and sign the connection symbol (bridge symbol) once?"

The answer to this question is that this approach will work; however, in this case the recipients will only receive 1% of the universal energy sent. It is essential to call in each person with the three symbols to be 100% effective in the transmission of the healing. This same law also applies for initiation procedures. It is worth noting here that if a teacher offers group attunements, one should be somewhat discriminating as a full Reiki attunement cannot be certain.

The Reiki Box

Another excellent way to send absent healing to many individuals, or wide scale situations like natural disasters, accidents, countries in conflict, political unrest, etc., is to send healing using the Reiki Box.

For this procedure, the practitioner needs a small box preferably made of natural materials. The preferred materials for a Reiki box are: wood, shell, crystal, bone, silver, copper or gold. These materials hold as well as amplify Reiki energy. Contained within the box are the people or situations that require healing.

In order to be most effective, each situation or person must be called in separately by signing the three Reiki Second Degree symbols over each person or situation. Photos of the individuals are useful; however, if they are not available then the recipients' full name and where they live will suffice. Once all are called in, we send healing to the box, with each hand on either side, sending healing energy to the situations and people concerned.

A more general approach is to call everyone into the box at the calling in stage. Here one does not state each person separately, one just states a general invocation. We then draw the symbols once for all concerned. This simplified version sends just one stream of energy to the group instead of several separate streams. For example if there were 10 people's names or photos in the box, then each person would only receive 10% each of the healing energy. This method works particularly well for geographical locations that require healing, like a forest needing protection or a country at war.

As the box is used on a continual basis, the energy will build more and more. These boxes can really become a beacon of healing energy. After some time, a person need only put a photo in the box for that individual to receive healing energy and a blessing. It is for this reason that natural materials are recommended, as they hold and accumulate energy better than synthetic materials.

Sending Healing to our Inner Child

Most of our adult lives are lived out of our conditioned experiences from childhood. This occurs usually in our formative years, approximately from birth until age 7. It is at this age that we form base concepts of our outer world, in particular, how to receive affection, validation, and love. It is often from the denial of love that stems our wounding and resultantly, our dysfunctional responses that we live out in our relationships and interactions with others as adults.

Sending healing to the archetype of our inner child can be rewarding, sometimes confronting and often insightful in the healing of old patterns.

The procedure follows the same procedure, as before, with the only difference being the calling in stage. For example: After accessing with the Sei Heki, calling: "Myself at age five, myself at age five, myself at age five, Am I there?" Then proceeding with the three symbols to bridge the healing.

It is generally suggested that people use a teddy bear as a proxy, as this symbolically represents holding yourself as a child. This process can often bring up varied emotional responses in people. Such as: tears, sadness, joy or play. Most people experience this practice to be a very gentle way to touch a deep part of their being. It is very healing to hold ourselves as children, and comfort the unloved parts of ourselves.

A further extension of this is to send an Absent Healing to your inner child, with each day representing a year of your life. The practitioner sends Absent Healing each day consecutively until the current age is met. In effect one is healing ones life. By facilitating this process for each consecutive year, the energy squares itself and becomes an accumulation of power each day.

The only drawback is, the older you are in years, the longer this process will take to complete. The way to facilitate this process is to begin by sending absent healing to your conception. This is the time when your fathers' sperm and your mothers egg joined and it is at this time when your consciousness formed into a physical form. The following day send an Absent Healing from the time between your conception to your birth. The following day you send a healing to your birth. Then the following day you send a healing to the time from your birth to your first birthday, then from your first birthday until your second and so on until your present age. One continues healing in this manner until each year has been sent an Absent Healing. If you have a time in your past where you know something has happened which causes obstacles in your adult life, then one can focus on this particular time, until some change is indicated.

Sending Healing to Past Issues

Sending healing to the past is a beneficial way to heal current issues that we have as adults.

The method used here is the calling in of an issue and stating that the healing energy is sent to the origin of the issue. During the procedure, the practitioner will state: 'I am now sending healing energy to the root cause of the issue which I have with (state the issue).' This is stated three times and healing energy is sent to this time. With this procedure, we do not need to know the year the origin of the issue was formed, because by simply calling in the origin of the issue and bridging with the symbols, the Divine Intelligence of the Reiki energy will go to that time and heal whatever is most appropriate.

In other cases, we may know the specific date, month or year that an agenda was formed, and if this is the case, we call in this time as our reference point.

A question that sometimes comes up with regard to healing past issues is, 'Why can't I send healing to all my issues from the past that affect me now, in one healing?' The response to this is, yes you can, but the effectiveness of your approach would be like trying to melt an iceberg with a magnifying glass. The more appropriate approach is to send healing to specific issues, and perhaps send healing to an issue every day for several days. Sometimes one healing is sufficient to heal an issue, and other times it is an ongoing process. By specializing in a particular area, we pull all our resources into one place and our effectiveness is therefore much greater.

Sending Healing Energy into the Future

When sending healing into the future, we apply the same principles and methods used to send healing to the past. The only dif-

ference is the calling stage and what is stated. If, for example, we
wished to send Absent Healing to a court case for ourselves or
someone else, we could do the following: We could send healing to
the judge so that he would be in a good and moral space, and to
each person at the hearing. If we didn't know exactly what time of
the day the hearing was, then all that is required is to state that the
energy activates the moment you walk into the court room or
words to this effect. It is sufficient to direct healing energy into the
future and it is not necessary to know the specific linear time or
location for that matter. It can be activated by a cue of some kind.

   Another example would be sending healing energy to a future
exam, so that you would be calm, clear and recall all the material
necessary. If perhaps the exam is delayed or postponed for another
day, then the energy simply carries over to when a specific cue is
put in place. Your cue could be when you pick up your pen at the
beginning of the exam, then, the energy is activated for your highest good.

   Sending healing into the future can bring together all the elements in a situation to work in your favor. This is by no means the
manipulation of circumstances, as the Reiki energy is always set
with the highest intent: 'For the benefit of all concerned', or, 'This
or something better be done'.

   Through sending healing energy and symbols to future events,
we remove any obstacles that prevents flow and assists in promoting harmony.

   Some other examples of future situations are: to send healing to
a journey, flight or car ride, a business meeting, a seminar, a job
interview, a holiday, a party, a wedding, a funeral, a work environment, etc.

   Sending healing to future events also secures a location from
any negative influences that may otherwise create a disturbance in
the natural order of things.

Sending Healing to Situations
of Conflict and Crises

Absent Healing can be invaluable in times of great distress, anxiety
or emergencies. When we are faced with dire circumstances, we
often do not know what to do.

   In these situations we can apply Absent Healing. This is still effective even if we are not present or even know the individual or
individuals' involved. An example of this may be driving past a
road accident. We simply call in the situation, all the people con-

cerned, even if we don't know the names, it is enough to state: "The woman injured in the crash", stating this three times and using the symbols to bridge the healing. Another example may be when we see a person in distress or feeling anxiety. In doing so we are sending pure unconditional love to soothe and calm the person concerned.

Sending Absent Healing to Two People at the Same Time

This procedure uses the body as a proxy to direct healing energy to two people simultaneously. The practice is ideal for relationships in conflict, whether this is between a couple, a father and son, a falling out between friends, etc.

The Procedure:

1. Follow the usual procedures of setting up boundaries and centering.
2. Using both hands, call in the first individual, stating their name three times. Once you have a connection, sign or visualize the three symbols in sequence.
3. Using your body as the proxy, now transfer this energy to your left knee.
4. Remembering that one part of your body needs to maintain contact throughout the absent healing procedure, slide your elbow down to your knee to maintain your contact and to free up your hands for the next stage.
5. Now with your hands free once again, yet still leaning your elbow on your left knee (which is person one), call in the second person in the traditional manner, three times, establish connection and sign or visualize the three symbols.
6. Now transfer the second person to your right knee as the proxy.
7. Slide your left hand down to your knee once again.
8. Now think to your self that one knee represents one person, and your other knee represents the other person. As long as your hands are on the proxy's, healing energy is being sent simultaneously in two streams of energy.
9. Turn your attention to your left knee and using internal dialogue ask the question, 'what does this person need to heal the conflict at hand?' (State the situation). Sign whichever symbols come to mind and direct healing energy to the person and to the areas where they are carrying the emotional pain of the conflict.

120 REIKI HEALER

The Type of Crystal

Quartz based crystals are generally best for healing work, especially clear quartz; however, any crystal you feel particularly drawn to can be used with good results. The thing to remember is that a crystal has its own energy field and that energy field will have a specific effect on the energy field of a person. Therefore, before we use a crystal on another, we first need to determine its suitability. We also need to consider whether it has been purified from prior handling. We then need to know how to program the crystal for healing and how to maintain this vibration for future use.

The size of the crystal is not that important. Some people believe that the bigger the crystal, the greater the healing properties will be. On the other hand, some people consider the clarity of the crystal to be the most important factor and this too is not so relevant as a personal connection is what matters most.

Purification of the Crystal

Once you have a crystal you are happy with, you will need to cleanse it from previous people who have handled it or programmed it. A crystal is like a sponge and absorbs energy from its surrounding environment. This includes negative as well as positive influences.

To purify a crystal, use natural spring water or better still a natural spring, river or lake. One can use water and natural earth to wash the crystal or place it in the earth. A common 'New Age' misconception is using salt water to cleanse crystals. Quartz Crystals don't grow out of the ocean, so it makes sense to use elements that are natural to a crystal's environment. Salt water can be quite damaging to the energy field of the crystal and should be avoided when possible.

Once we have purified the crystal in water, we can energize the crystal on a full moon overnight. This will energize the crystal and establish a balance with the energies of sky and earth.

Now that our crystal is clear, we are ready to work with it for Absent Healing. The following is a general outline.

The Programming of the Crystal for Absent Healing

After you have washed the crystal and charged its energies with the elements and the sun and moon, hold the crystal in your hands and clear the crystal, using the following clearing exercise.

Pass the Sei Heki through the crystal three times, stating that any lesser or lower energies now leave this crystal and only the highest energies remain, and that all is transformed into the highest good. This can be done by signing the symbol over the crystal and imagining it moving through the crystal, clearing any lower energy.

Now we are ready to program the crystal with any intent we desire.

Sign the three symbols as in an Absent Healing procedure: Honsha Ze Shonen, Sei Heki, Choku Rei. Now state clearly and precisely your intent for the crystal, stating this three times and blowing a Choku Rei into the crystal. One should do this after each intention is stated. Take a few minutes to generate your intention.

Once you feel this is complete, sign the three symbols again over the crystal and blow through the crystal and cupped hands three times. This activates the program.

Care and Maintenance of an Absent Healing Crystal

It is best to only let yourself handle the crystal, to keep the vibrations aligned to your energy field. This is not for any superstitious reasons it is merely a way to keep the energies of the crystal aligned with your energy field.

A way to maintain your crystal is to cleanse it after each Absent Healing with either a Smudge Stick (Sage smoke) or by using the Sei Heki clearing exercise. In addition to this it is good to leave your crystal under moonlight in nature every month to allow it to absorb the frequencies from the elements of nature.

Another way to maintain the positive qualities of the crystal is to ask your Reiki teacher to give the crystal a Reiki attunement. In this way the crystal becomes a beacon or channel for healing energy and will be better maintained for healing work.

How to Use Crystals for Absent Healing

Using crystals is especially good for Absent Healing as they magnify the intent and Reiki energy. If you have a crystal for Absent Healing use it as the proxy and keep the purpose of the crystal only for healing work. This will build up the intent over time and contain the energy for that specific purpose.

To use the crystal for Absent Healing, we use it as the proxy or effigy to represent the situation or person requiring healing. The more we use it, the more energy we build. In time, these crystals can become very powerful and can hold healing properties with regular use.

Using crystals on the body or in hands-on healing sessions is generally an unnecessary extension to traditional Reiki. If you are intent on the use of crystals in healing, be certain to gain reliable training in this field, as it is important to know what you are doing. If you do intend to use crystals in Reiki as part of hands on healing, it is better to keep their use reasonably well hidden. One way is to keep the crystal in your pocket or around your neck. This will amplify your energy field.

The reason we keep their use fairly covert is that if you are waving a crystal around someone's energy field, a new person to Reiki might get the wrong impression thinking that, "Reiki, oh yeah that's all about using crystals for healing." Reiki is Reiki, so there is no need to create confusion around the system when it is complete in and of itself.

Also avoid using crystal layouts on the body in your healing work. It is vitally important to have a solid knowledge on how the crystal's energy field interacts with the human energy field. Ideally, we should be presenting Reiki in a way that holds true to the original practice.

Unless you have a complete knowledge of this practice, it is best to leave it alone as you will more than likely cause a misalignment in another's energy field, rather than a healing effect.

CHAPTER TWELVE

'The heart is to the body what the sun is to the world'.

— SRI RAMANA MAHARSHI

The Chakras

The word Chakra (Sanskrit), Cakkhu (Pali) means: wheel, center, eye, and energy nexus within the subtle energy body. The Chakras are the basis of the energetic structure of the human being. These energy centers stem along a central axis point (central channel) that runs from the crown Chakra to the base of the body.

The Chakras are a vital link to the totality of our being. Each center represents the myriad aspects of who we are. Working with these sources of energy can assist in our personal growth, well-being and personal development.

Each Chakra vibrates at a specific frequency and is affected by light, color and sound. The Chakras can be affected by these means and other vibrational frequencies. These frequencies affect the Chakras by means of sympathetic resonance.

The Chakra system also corresponds to the endocrine system of the body. The endocrine system controls the hormonal balance within human beings and it is these hormones that have a strong effect on our emotions as individuals.

In the case where one or many of our Chakras are out of balance, then this will also effect our endocrine system and as a result, our emotional body. This is why the method of Chakra balancing can be very beneficial in balancing the body, mind and emotions.

There are many schools of thought about the Chakras. In this example we will illustrate the system that is a common model in most eastern spiritual traditions.

The Chakra System

1. The Base Chakra

The base Chakra is situated at the base of the body at the perineum muscle. The base Chakra governs the supply of energy to the reproductive organs, the kidneys, the adrenal glands and spinal column. The base Chakra relates to our will to live, survival, procreation, family law, fight-flight response and our basic human instincts. The corresponding color is red.

2. The Sacral Chakra (Hara Chakra)

This Chakra is situated three finger widths below the belly button and stems from the front and back of the central channel. It is related to our emotions of sensuality and sexuality. The sacral is related to our drive in the physical world, and supplies our immune system and sexual organs with additional power. The sacral Chakra is the seat of our personal power. The corresponding color is orange.

3. The Solar Plexus Chakra

The solar plexus Chakra is situated where the rib cage meets in the lower chest. Like the sacral Chakra, it protrudes from the front and back of the body. This Chakra is related to issues of personal power, self-esteem/self image and our emotional selves. It is linked to the gall bladder, the digestive system and the pancreas. The corresponding color is yellow.

4. The Heart Chakra

The heart Chakra is located in the center of our chest, this center governs our ability to give and receive love. Here is the seat of compassion, giving, self-sacrifice, and unconditional love. The heart Chakra governs the heart, the thymus gland, the circulatory system and lungs. The corresponding color is green or pink.

5. The Throat Chakra

The throat Chakra is located in the centre of the throat and protrudes from back and front of the neck. This centre governs communication and our ability to speak our truth or to voice our opinions. The corresponding color is blue.

6. The Brow Chakra

This Chakra is located at the center of our brow, between our eyebrows and the original hairline. This Chakra protrudes from the front and back of the head and governs our intuition and intellect. It is the active center of our imagination and our abilities of intuition, clairvoyance and psychic sensitivity. This Chakra also relates to our pituitary and pineal glands. The corresponding color is indigo.

7. The Crown Chakra

The crown Chakra is located eight finger widths from the original hairline and is directly vertical to the tips of the ears when drawn directly upwards. The crown Chakra governs our attributes of spiritual potential and universal understanding. Other related factors include, wisdom, clarity, oneness, unity and the interconnectedness with all life. It is our source to life and the activation point of the Reiki energy. The corresponding colors are purple, gold or white.

Chakra Balancing

Balancing the Chakras with the Reiki symbols

The Chakras or energy centers of the body are major storehouses of information relating to our physical, psychological, emotional, and psycho-spiritual selves. In relation to healing, the Chakras give us a clear map of the overall health of a person on an energetic level.

During a session we may need to balance a Chakra or a series of Chakras. By applying symbols and energy to each individual Chakra, we greatly assist in creating balance throughout the energy body.

Procedure:

1. Draw HONSHA ZE SHONEN over the Crown Chakra.
2. Draw SEI HEKI over the Crown Chakra.
3. Draw CHOKU REI over the Crown Chakra.

- Place palm over palm, doubling the hand Chakras over each energy center.
- Visualize each symbol (steps 1 to 3) and leave the hands at the Chakra point for approximately 5 to 10 minutes.
- Now repeat the whole process for each following Chakra: Brow, Throat, Heart, Solar Plexus, Sacral, and Base Chakras.

It is recommended that the practitioner access the recipient with the Sei Heki to determine whether the person has received enough energy at each point. During a session it may be that only a few points may require balancing; however, as a sequence this procedure aligns the individual and deeply touches the core of each center and our being. Therefore we balance each center from the crown to the base.

This is a very powerful technique for balancing the Chakras. It can be used instead of a full treatment or for one's self-healing. It can also be combined into your hands-on sessions and absent healing procedures.

To finish a session, ground your client by gently massaging both feet and allow them some time to come around.

Chakra Balancing as a Self-treatment

The same procedure that we use on another can also be applied to ourselves. This process deepens our connection with our center and establishes a deep calm throughout the process.

We begin in the following manner:

Procedure:

1. Draw HONSHA ZE SHONEN over your crown Chakra.

2. Draw SEI HEKI over your crown Chakra.

3. Draw CHOKU REI over your crown Chakra.

• Place palm over palm, doubling the hand Chakras over each energy center.

• Visualize each symbol (steps 1 to 3) and leave the hands at the Chakra point for approximately 5 to 10 minutes.

• Now repeat the whole process for each Chakra center. Brow, Throat, Heart, Solar Plexus, Sacral, and Base Chakras.

As we are working on the energy centers, many people report a difference in the feelings and results of these sessions. Many people also report a greater depth achieved through the hands on sessions and a centeredness that follows, often for days.

Life Mapping through the Chakras

This method is a direct way of healing the underlying issues that shape the way we act and react in our lives. Through the techniques of body focusing and hands on healing, we can ascertain the dominant issues within each energy center and actively change our relationship to these issues.

This process is facilitated by breath work, visualization, body awareness and internal dialogue to pinpoint the issue in mind.

This technique is useful when we are faced with obstacles which are unknown or obscured by our emotions. It is also a good method for times when we need renewed clarity and direction in our healing path.

The process is as follows:

1. This exercise involves two people, a facilitator and a recipient.

2. The recipient lies down with their eyes closed and relaxes, and the facilitator sits beside the person with a note pad and pen.

3. Now the facilitator asks the recipient to breathe into and focus their awareness on their base Chakra. The recipient places their hands on their base Chakra, hands on the pubic bone, palm over palm as in the Chakra balancing technique. * NOTE: The facilitator does not apply the hands to the recipient.

4. The recipient breathes into this area. The facilitator asks the key question to the recipient and asks the recipient to say to themselves inwardly 'Am I safe?' or 'How can I be safe?'

5. The recipient is then asked to speak whatever sense impressions come to mind in relation to the question. These can be images, thoughts, feelings, sensations, dialogue, etc. The idea is to speak the immediate impressions without analyzing them. The process encourages intuitive responses.

6. As the recipient speaks these impressions, the facilitator writes them down for future reference, making sure to clarify and read back anything that was not heard clearly.

7. A few sentences is sufficient and the facilitator directs the recipient to drop the awareness in this area and to turn the focused awareness on their sacral Chakra or Hara. Following the same process as before, the recipient places their hands on their Hara. The facilitator asks the question: 'What is my personal power?' or 'Do I know and use my personal power effectively?' Speaking their immediate impressions, the facilitator writes these impressions down as before.

8. This process is repeated for the following Chakras with the key questions being: Solar Plexus Chakra: 'Am I worthy?' or 'How can I be worthy?'

9. Heart Chakra: 'Do I give and receive love?' or 'How can I give and receive love?'

10. Throat Chakra: 'Do I express myself?' or 'How can I express myself?'

11. Brow Chakra: 'What do I need to know?' or 'Do I know what is necessary for me?'

12. Crown Chakra: 'What is my spiritual path?' or 'How can I walk my spiritual path?'

Once the facilitator has moved through this process, the recipient remains with their eyes closed and relaxed and the recipient reads back what was spoken. As this is being done, the recipient places their hands on the corresponding Chakras. With their hands once more on each center the recipient may add any further impressions that may arise from these areas as a result of reading back the prior material.

Once this is complete, the recipient looks at the information and together the recipient and facilitator try to encapsulate these sentences into one phrase or word that summarizes the impressions. The idea is to contain each Chakra with a particular phrase or 'key code'; meaning the key to unlock the code lying within the Chakra. In mapping the Chakras in this way, the individual has a direct insight into their overall energetic make up. Some energy centers may be negative in their summary, and some may be life giving and positive.

An example to give you some idea might be something along the lines of:

Facilitator: "Am I worthy?"

Recipient: "I feel a tightness in my chest, like someone is sitting on it. It reminds me of being locked inside a room. The room is dark, I cannot see a way out" etc...

Summary: "I feel suppressed"

This example is only a fabrication, and the idea is to determine a key phrase that one can then use for Absent Healing. When this process of elimination has been determined, the issue or 'code' can be the focus of Absent Healing or hands on healing. One can use these codes as the calling in stage in Absent Healing. For example: "I am now calling in my issue of feeling suppressed", on the other hand we can focus the issue to the physical body and apply hands on healing to the area where the issue resides.

CHAPTER THIRTEEN

'When you are strong and healthy,
you never think of sickness coming.
But it descends with sudden force, like a strike of lightening.'

— MILAREPA

Setting up your own Reiki practice

After successfully completing the necessary practice of Reiki Second Degree, many students take the first steps towards setting up their own Reiki practice. The following suggestions are some helpful guidelines for setting up your own Reiki practice.

- Consider how you will promote yourself: advertising, flyers, information evenings, presentations and talks, editorials in magazines, health and lifestyle expos or referral in conjunction with other health practitioners.
- Consider establishing a professional session room. You may consider hiring a room or working from home. Is the space you have at home conducive to healing or would leasing a room be more appropriate for your practice?
- Will you take out public liability insurance?
- What fee will you charge for your services and will this be enough at the end of the day to make a profit?

As part of being a practitioner, it is wise to consider how one conducts oneself in a healing situation. At all times it is best to present yourself and your art in a professional and clear way. When we are facilitating a session for another we should endeavor to make our client as comfortable as possible. Part of this is to convey clearly what we are presenting and what they might expect from the session. A simple thing to ask once you have explained the process is whether they have any questions. This gives the person the opportunity to ask questions and it will also confirm for you that they have at least a basic understanding of the healing process.

Please refer to the IIRT Code of Ethics in chapter 18. These simple codes are a solid foundation and guide to the practice of Reiki.

Creating a Space Conducive to Healing

When circumstances permit it is ideal to set up a room that is tailored to your Reiki practice.

Rooms that help generate positive energy are generally, well-lit with natural sun light, well-ventilated, i.e., with windows and are uncluttered in their arrangement. A simple, ordered and clean room will naturally attract positive influences. To enhance this further, you may wish to set up an altar of sacred objects that have meaning for you. Often a candle is a nice touch.

Setting a shrine gives a focus of intent to a room and will naturally enhance the vibration you are working with. The idea is to keep it simple. Less is more!

Before commencing a session be sure to take the phone off the hook. Let others that may be sharing your space with you know that you will need the allotted time to be relatively quiet.

If you have any pets such as cats or dogs, take them out of the room as animals love Reiki and may distract your session.

These guidelines help to support a Reiki session but they are not completely essential to be effective in your treatments. Reiki can be done anywhere and at anytime. Regardless of disturbing influences within the environment, the healing taking place is still the same. Don't limit the time or places where you practice Reiki. Sometimes circumstances prevent the perfect settings from being available. The idea is to do the best with what you have at any given moment.

Being a Living Example of Reiki

The point of informing clients about what you are doing is important. As practitioners of Reiki part of our responsibility is to educate. This is why we need to present ourselves to the public with a view that supports a moral, ethical and grounded approach to healing. It is therefore important to make clear distinctions between what is Reiki and what is being incorporated into the modality. This is a responsibility each Reiki practitioner holds. If a client shows an interest in learning, refer them to a good teacher or offer them information and further details from your personal experience with Reiki. Although many who have learned are inspired with Reiki's benefits, it is not the role of the Reiki practitioner to convert anyone to Reiki. The best way to inspire others is to be a living example of Reiki in your life. That way they will see your positive changes and will ask you things like: "Wow, you seem to be much calmer these days", or "Now you seem to be a nicer person, what happened?"

Living by example is one of the best advertisements for Reiki. Reiki is a path by being. Then our walk will do the talking and we will not feel the need to convert the so called 'unconverted'.

Another important point to mention is the responsibility that each Practitioner holds to their client. Reiki is a path of service to another. You are there to serve your client, not your own ideas of how great a healer you can be. Remember that your client has come to you for help and that it is your obligation to do your best to heal them and to uphold the Reiki tradition in a respectful and dignified manner. The further we progress along a spiritual path, the more we need to surrender to humility. After all, service is the quick path.

How Much Should I Charge for Reiki?

Many people feel uncomfortable with charging a set rate for their healing services. And certainly it is hard to set a price on universal energy. Another way to look at this is in terms of our time and energy. To facilitate a Reiki session we need to set aside time and create a space for our prospective client, as well as preparing both physically, mentally and psychically for the session. Most practitioners charge the same as a regular massage therapist. If however you feel uncomfortable with this, facilitating Reiki for some other service or exchange is also a nice way to go. The bottom line is to value this sacred gift, and to value our self as a vehicle for this energy. It is also important to recognize our concepts of abundance and the values we place on things. There is no spiritual law that says we cannot be spiritual and earn a living. At the end of the day, our time is our time and this should be compensated by something in return. Be this money or some other form of exchange, we need to eat and we still have to pay the bills. If we neglect to create a space for exchange, be it in the form of money or other services, we can actually cause a karmic debt in the very person we are trying to heal. If we have no space for return for services rendered, the situation becomes unbalanced and this can cause obstacles to a path of healing. So the importance of exchange cannot be stressed enough, it is vital to a system of balance and maintaining a path which is in the spirit of generosity.

Requirements for a Second Degree Workshop

As outlined for the First Degree, a Second Degree class should cover the following:

1. One Reiki II Initiation, preferably at the beginning of the workshop.
2. The three Reiki II symbols are given, explained, practiced and memorized throughout the workshop.
3. At least one full hands-on session using the Reiki symbols during the workshop.
4. Methods of Absent Healing are explored and practiced in a variety of forms.
5. Using symbols to clear rooms is explained, demonstrated and practiced.
6. Personal boundaries, clearing and related centering procedures are demonstrated and practiced.
7. Practice requirements are given during and after the workshop.
8. Explanation of the Reiki II initiation and its empowerment for the Reiki II symbols.
9. Students receive a manual of procedures, symbols and techniques.
10. Students receive a certificate in Second Degree Reiki upon completion.
11. Total workshop duration: 12 hours.

CHAPTER FOURTEEN

*'Miracles are fantastic events which utilize hidden laws of
nature that most people are not aware of. Miracles do not break
the laws of nature, they are actually based on them.'*

— MASTER CHOA KOK SUI

Advanced Reiki

Extensions and Explorations Beyond
the Traditional Reiki II Level

At the International Institute for Reiki Training we offer training in
several Reiki styles and traditions. Part of our exploration with
Reiki has also been the development of additional practices that a
student may learn. Although Advanced Reiki is not a traditional
level, it has proven to be very beneficial in fine-tuning and extending on the principles taught in Reiki levels First and Second Degree.

In Advanced Reiki we extend beyond Reiki II into areas such as:

- Developing clairvoyant abilities.
- Methods for intuitive and psychic healing.
- Practices for working in the human energy field (aura).
- Buddhist perspectives on death and dying.
- Buddhist archetypes for healing (Medicine Buddha, meditation
  and practice).
- Absent healing for numerous situations (the healing triad).
- Working with inner guidance and extending healing methods on
  more expansive levels.

Advanced Reiki was implemented as a workshop to explore Reiki
in its myriad forms. As there is often not enough time to devote to
all the areas and ways that Reiki can be applied in a seminar, this

seminar offers the student the ground to explore these additional practices. This workshop is also a useful addition for Reiki students who already combine Reiki with other modalities.

To stress this point once again, Advanced Reiki is not a traditional Reiki level. It is an extension and elaboration of material from Reiki Second Degree.

In the following chapter we will explore some of these methods and how these can benefit an established practitioner.

The Quantum Healing Bank

As the name suggests, the Quantum Bank refers to a place where healings and symbols can be stored and later drawn upon at will or activated at specific times during healing sessions. As we know the Honsha Ze Shonen enables healing to be directed over time and space. With the Quantum Healing Bank we can put a time delay on healings and their transmission.

The Quantum Healing Bank is best imagined as a bubble or energy field above one's head. This energy field contains an abundance of healing energy and Reiki symbols that can be accessed by the practitioner at anytime for the healing of oneself or another.

Some of the applications of the Quantum Healing Bank:

1. Reiki symbols can be stored for direct use by the practitioner during a healing session or in Absent Healing, which can be activated in past, present or future situations.
2. Healings can be activated for oneself or another at specific times when using the Reiki Absent Healing sequence.
3. Healings can be duplicated and repeated over a series of hours, days, or weeks.
4. Healings or symbols can be directed to particular locations for a future time and space or for past situations.
5. A healing bank can be set up for a client so that they can consciously request healing energy at any time.

How to set up a Quantum Healing Bank

1. State the person's name three times and sign or visualize the Sei Heki at the crown of your client.
2. Determine how many symbols or how much healing energy is required and state when this will activate.
3. Seal this intent with a Choku Rei over the crown.

An Example:

Internally the dialogue is as follows: Visualize drawing the Sei

Heki. 'John, John, John, Do you require any additional healing or symbols?'

Recipient: 'Yes, healing every evening from the time that I go to sleep to the time that I wake up, for the following three nights.'

Facilitator: 'May this be for your highest good', visualize drawing a Choku Rei.

To seal this intent, you may blow the Choku Rei or infuse this into or just above the crown of the recipient.

Note: The Quantum Healing Bank needs to be attended to on a regular basis. For example, one could not set up a Quantum Healing Bank for themselves to receive healings every night at a specific time for the rest of their lives. The purpose for the bank is to focus healing intent, and the bank is a storage facility and vehicle for this energy transmission. Ideally for ongoing healings the bank should be set up once or twice a week. Ideally it should be set at the end of each healing session.

The Second Degree Booster Attunement

As with First Degree Reiki, the Second Degree has a particular attunement process that can boost the Second Degree practitioners' energy.

The Booster attunement serves as a way of experiencing the power of the Reiki energy and to enhance the energy flow within a practitioners' energy field.

During a Reiki attunement, a tremendous amount of positive healing energy is bestowed upon and through an individual. Receiving a Booster attunement is a direct way to enhance our energy fields' resonance.

The Reiki II Booster attunement serves this end by activating the three Reiki symbols that are given at the Reiki II level. Receiving and giving an attunement is also an empowering and pleasant experience as we are touched each time by the spiritual power and blessing of the Reiki energy.

Releasing the Ties that Bind

Releasing the ties that bind is a unique process to release oneself or another from situations of conflict or old relationships. It is also applicable for people who have died where there were unresolved issues or where one never had a chance to say goodbye.

This process allows forgiveness to follow as one is energetically and emotionally released from the situation.

There are often times in life where we hold onto past experiences, relationships or loved ones that should have been released years before, yet we feel bound to the past. Some of these factors may be purely emotional, other times it is the energy ties which are actually still connected to our energy body. These are the ties that we feel tugging at our 'heart strings'. On occasion this can also be experienced where someone else is invading our psychic space.

The following process assists in all of the above examples and is a direct way to release ourselves from situations we no longer need.

The procedure is as follows:

1. Call in the person as in the absent healing procedure.
2. Call the person's name three times, cupping your hands and draw or visualize: Honsha Ze Shonen, Sei Heki, Choku Rei.
3. Once you have established a connection transfer this thought form to a proxy of your choice. (You may want to transfer this to a piece of paper.)
4. State the situation three times, detailing the issues and your de-sired resolve to the current or past situation.
5. Now state the following: (state the person's name three times, then say:) *'I fully and freely release you and let you go to the Divine Intelligence, whose perfect work is in you and flows through you. I forgive you and I forgive myself. I am free and you are free and all is cleansed and released between us both now and in the future.'*
6. Sign in the air in front of you a large Sei Heki. Imagine this is cutting the energy ties between your body and theirs. This is visualized as cords of energy between you and the person con-cerned.
7. Now repeat steps 4 to 6.
8. Repeat steps 4 to 6 once more.
9. Once you have completed this sequence three times, visualize this person/situation symbolically fading off into the distance or reducing in size until it has completely disappeared. Give thanks in your own way for the release of this situation and the lessons that were presented at the time.
10. Now burn the paper that was your proxy, stating that no harm comes to the individual concerned.
11. Close the absent healing in the traditional manner by drawing the Choku Rei and blowing through cupped hands three times to complete the healing process.

This technique may be repeated on a regular basis or until the issue subsides.

The Reiki Healing Triad

The Healing Triad is an extension on the concepts of absent healing. It incorporates Sacred Geometry, the Choku Rei symbol, the elements of the situation, its outcome and the outer forces that come into play.

Healing Triads are particularly useful in addressing situations where there is more than one person involved to actively remove obstacles to one's healing.

Healing Triads can be used in three ways. Firstly as an absent healing procedure, utilizing a particular mudra (hand gesture). Secondly as a visualization, and thirdly as a physical proxy; applying the practice to the geometry of the physical body. To follow the latter example, the student can effectively facilitate absent healing on the recipient while performing a hands on session. But first let us illustrate the absent healing procedure.

Absent Healing Triad

The procedure is as follows:

1. Think of an issue or obstacle in your life. Have with you a reasonable sized piece of paper and a pen.
2. Draw a large triangle on the page, big enough for you to put your hands in. Physically draw a Choku Rei inside the triangle at each corner.
3. Now write these issues or what you wish to manifest, in a clear and direct manner at the center of the triangle.
4. Call in the issue that requires healing between your hands, stating this three times and sign the Honsha Ze Shonen, Sei Heki and Choku Rei, then transfer your hands to the proxy, which in this case is the piece of paper.
5. Turn your attention to the left hand corner of the triangle and write the current issue. Include all the people involved as well as the location or situation. This area of the triangle represents the current situation.
6. Now turn your attention to the right hand corner of the triangle and write your desired outcome, including the people involved.
7. The upper corner of the triangle is left blank. This area represents the Universal healing energy as well as all the outer forces that would help in this situation.
8. Now begin your absent healing in the usual manner, calling in the issue in the standard procedure.
9. Once the symbols have been signed and you have contact, trans-

fer your hands to the proxy. Place your hands on the paper in the lower left hand corner (the current situation). Sign symbols intuitively and direct healing energy to the people and situation that is current. Send for approximately five minutes.

10. Now turn your attention on the lower right hand corner and sign any symbols needed and direct healing energy to the people concerned and situation for your ideal outcome. Send for five minutes.

11. Lastly, place your hands on the upper section of the triangle. Send healing energy to all those that would help.

12. Once you have finished, fold each corner into the center. Firstly, the left hand corner to the center, then the right hand corner to the center and finally the upper corner to the center. Here we bring all the elements together, combining and igniting this power. Hold this now between your hands for a short time until it feels complete.

13. Once you have completed this procedure blow the Choku Rei through your hands and the folded paper three times to release the healing process.

You may choose to burn this Mandala or keep it in a special place. When you burn the healing triad you symbolically release yourself from the situation and your attachments to the outcome.

Visualizing the Triad

This procedure can also be visualized by forming a triad with your hands. This is done by placing your thumbs and index fingers together to form a triangle. The person holds this mudra in front of them or over their own brow Chakra. One then calls to mind the people and situations involved. The symbols are drawn with the tip of your nose and directed with your eyes. These can be blown with the breath into the areas required by following the procedure before.

Healing Triads on the Body

While performing hands on healing, one can use the healing triad on specific points on the body. The left foot represents the left hand corner of the triad, the right foot represents the right hand corner of the triad and the crown Chakra represents the top of the triad.

Here the facilitator signs a Choku Rei for each corner. One symbol on the left foot, one on the right foot and one on the crown of the head. Now following the steps as before one brings all of these points together at the heart Chakra of the individual and signing the symbol over the whole body to close.

Healing Triads and Chakras

This process can also be used on one specific point or Chakra of an individual. Once a Chakra has been identified as requiring healing energy, this Chakra becomes the proxy of the process.

Here the facilitator places their hands on the Chakra concerned and forms the triad with their thumbs and index fingers joined.

The Healing triad procedure is then visualized from this point to resolve the root cause of the issue determined from the life mapping through the Chakras process from chapter 12. This process can be repeated for subsequent Chakras or other areas in need.

CHAPTER FIFTEEN

*'One single torch can dissipate the accumulated darkness
of a thousand eons. Likewise, a single instant of
clear light in mind eliminates the ignorance
and obscurations accumulated over countless eons.'*

— *TILOPA*, MAHAMUDRA OF THE GANGES

Reiki and Buddhism

It is clear from recent research that the origins of Reiki are based on the practices of Buddhism. As an introduction, the following are some of the ways that the practitioner of Reiki can utilize some of the introductory Buddhist practices to enhance their own healing practice. One does not need to be Buddhist to practice these techniques, although formal commitments to the teachings are preferable as this level of trust in these methods opens a practitioner to be more able to generate positive results in healing. Many practitioners who wish to gain a deeper connection to these teachings should seek a good Buddhist Lama and take Buddhist Refuge and the necessary initiations.

Buddhist Refuge can be explained in the following way. Refuge represents a trust in the goal of enlightenment for the benefit of all beings, the way or teachings that take us there and the community of friends of the path. Traditionally these are called the three refuges. Also called: The Three Jewels of Refuge. These being: The Buddha, The Dharma and The noble Sangha.

When we take refuge we make certain promises to the Buddha. Buddha is not a god or a person but represents our own potential for awakening which is the clear light and undying potential of our minds. This is a symbol of our aspiration to know ourselves better and to recognize that we all have the potential for awakening to our true Buddha nature.

Secondly, we take refuge in the Dharma. These are the teachings

of the Buddha. The ways or methods that lead our minds to liberation from ignorance. Through the methods that remove our obstacles, we learn to purify our minds and to generate spiritual understanding and healing.

Thirdly, we take refuge in the Sangha. The Sangha represents
the community of friends who support these teachings as well as
your own spiritual development. This includes fellow Dharma students, the Lama (Spiritual teacher) and all those who would help
us in gaining liberation.

To give a complete overview of the Buddhist teachings would
require a separate book in itself. If you have an interest in gaining
a sound understanding and general overview of the Buddhist
path, one b ok I highly recommend is *Luminous Mind*, by Kalu
Rinpoche. The details for *Luminous Mind* can be found in the Bibli-
ography at the end of this book.

In light of this modest introduction, the following teachings are
some methods that a practitioner of Reiki can utilize for opening to
the healing potential of the Buddhist teachings.

Using Mantras with Reiki

Mantras are a sequence of syllables that hold particular frequencies for healing. In the Buddhist tradition perhaps the most widely
practiced mantra is: OM MANI PADME HUNG, the Buddha of
Compassion 'Avalokiteshvara' (Sanskrit) or Buddha 'Chenrezigi'
(Tibetan). The vibration of this mantra evokes the energy of the
unfolding heart of compassion. Its essential meaning is "all praise
to the unfolding of the jewel in the heart of the devoted". As with
all mantras, it is important to receive the transmission of this empowerment from a qualified Lama (Buddhist Master or Geshe) in
the form of a blessing (Loung) or initiation (Wonkur). However, if
this is not possible then it is permissible to use these mantras with
our Reiki or meditation practice and aim to at least receive this
blessing and Buddhist refuge sometime in the future.

The Buddha wants all beings to be free, regardless of position,
belief or virtue. This is one of the reasons why the Buddhist teachings are given out of compassion for anyone who desires to learn.

To use a mantra is an experience of repeating these syllables
over and over. By the repetitive invocation of these vibrations, we
evoke the vibration and energetic maps of the qualities we seek.
Mantras can be sung, spoken slowly or quickly. It is best to explore
which way feels appropriate for you. The more one repeats these
mantras, the greater qualities one gains, so it is best to do as many
as you can.

Some popular Buddhist Mantras and their meanings:

OM MANI PADME HUNG

Buddha name: Avalokiteshvara.

Archetypal Deity: Buddha of Loving Kindness and Compassion.

Mantra translation: Om Jewel of unfolding Hung.

OM AMI DEWA HRIH

Buddha name: Amitabha.

Archetypal Deity: Buddha of Limitless Light, Guardian of Dewachen (Pure realm).

Mantra translation: Om Lord of Limitless Light Hrih.

OM TARE TUTTARE TURE SOHA

Buddha name: Green Tara.

Archetypal Deity: Buddha of Great Liberation.

Mantra translation: Om Liberitous, Liberate now.

OM BENZA SATO HUNG

Buddha name: Dorje Sempa.

Archetypal Deity: Buddha of Purification (Diamond mind).

Mantra translation: Om Diamond Being Hung.

OM ARA PA CHA NA DHIH

Buddha name: Manjushri.

Archetypal Deity: Buddha of Wisdom.

Mantra translation: No translation literal in English.

Mantra Represents: 'Perfect Wisdom'.

OM GATE GATE PARAGATE PARASAMGATE BODHI SOHA

Buddha name: Prajinaparamita.

Archetypal Deity: Mother of all the Buddha's.

Mantra translation: Om gone, gone, gone completely beyond, awakening, let it happen.

TAYATA OM BHEKHANDZE BHEKHANDZE MAHA BHEKHANDZE BHEKHANDZE RANDZA SAMUNGATE SOHA

Buddha name: Sangle Mendela (Medicine Buddha).

Archetypal Deity: Buddha of Healing.

Mantra translation: Thus gone, healer, great healer King, accomplish healing, let it happen.

To receive empowerments for the various Buddhist archetypes contact your local Mahayana or Vajrayana Buddhist center.

Out of the main branches of Buddhism there are three main traditions, these being the vehicles of Hinayana, Mahayana and Vajrayana. These empowerments are mostly prominent in the Mahayana and Vajrayana schools of Tibetan Buddhism. The best way to keep informed of upcoming initiations for these archetypes is to be on the mailing lists or by attending meditation sessions at these centers.

Buddhist Archetypes

Some of the Archetypes described previously represent the vehicles of generating particular states of mind and the way to join with these energies.

The practice of these deities allows (particular to their use) the cultivation of certain positive qualities and the purification of obstacles. One should, where possible, gain a deeper understanding from the caring guidance of a qualified Lama. With right motivation, right understanding and the right methods, one can gain meaningful and lasting results.

Medicine Buddha, The Buddha of Healing

MEDICINE BUDDHA

The central deity that governs the system of Reiki is Medicine Buddha, the Buddha of Healing.

Medicine Buddha is a Buddhist Archetype popular in the Mahayana and Vajrayana Buddhist traditions. Medicine Buddha's practice is also very widespread throughout the Buddhist world. This practice has widespread popularity in Tibet, Nepal, Bhutan and in Japan's Shingon Buddhist tradition. Medicine Buddha is depicted in the color blue (Medicine Buddha's body), which in this practice represents the removal of physical disease, and a Gold robe, which represents the removal of mental, emotional and spiritual afflictions. In Tibetan Buddhism, Medicine Buddha is also referred to as 'Sangye Mendela', (King of lapis lazuli radiance). Medicine Buddha is depicted holding a begging bowl in his left hand and in his right hand in the mudra of generosity, holding the sacred herb, the Aurora plant or myrobalan (*Terminalia Chebula*); which is a well-known herb in Indian medicine. To evoke the qualities and healing energy of this deity, the following meditation is an excellent practice to achieve the union with the mind stream of Medicine Buddha.

Medicine Buddha Meditation

The procedure is as follows:

Motivation

Contemplate your own illnesses, past and present and the illnesses and pain experienced by others. Generate a strong desire to be free of this suffering and for all other sentient beings to likewise be free from all illness and injury.

Now think and affirm in your mind that you will commit yourself to invoking the healing power of Medicine Buddha to aid in the healing of illness and suffering for yourself and others. Having contemplated these, we have set the ground of right motivation and proceed with the meditation.

The Visualization

Visualize Medicine Buddha either above the crown of your head or the crown of the person who you wish to bestow healing upon. The Buddha is a tenth of our size and faces the same direction as the recipient or ourselves.

He is sitting upon a lotus seat and moon-colored cushion. He is radiant, translucent blue in color and his appearance is vibrant and beautiful. In his right hand he holds the Aurora plant in the mudra of supreme generosity. In his left hand is held a begging bowl. His bowl is colored blue on the outside and is white inside. The bowl contains all kinds of medicines and medicinal nectar. This nectar is the ambrosia of life and contains all herbs, minerals, healing powers and forces beyond the physical realm.

Prayer of Request

Now repeat the Prayer of Request: *"I strongly request to you Medi-*

cine Buddha, please grant me your blessing, that I may completely purify
my body, speech and mind. May I heal myself by developing my own
innate Medicine Buddha nature. I strongly request to you Medicine Bud-
dha, please bestow your blessing upon me, that I may completely alleviate
the suffering both mental and physical of every single sentient being."

Now imagine that Medicine Buddha is delighted by your sin-
cerity and requests. He now begins to emanate and radiate white
light that pours from his heart, skin and begging bowl. This light
pours like rain into our crown or the crown of another and completely fills our body and mind with this healing power. This light
completely purifies all our disease, afflictions, mental obstructions,
negative karma, emotional problems and negative feelings. See
your body and mind becoming clear, clean and pure.

While visualizing this purification, recite the Medicine Buddha
mantra 21 or 108 times:

TAYATA OM BHEKHANDZE BHEKHANDZE MAHA
BHEKHANDZE BHEKHANDZE RANDZA SAMUNGATE
SOHA

Now imagine that Medicine Buddha is emanating and radiating
lapis lazuli blue light. This blue light pours from his heart, skin and
begging bowl. This light pours like rain into our crown or the
crown of another and completely fills our body and mind with this
healing power. This blue light completely destroys all physical illness, disease and negative energies of the whole body. See your
body becoming energized, strong and clear.

While visualizing this transmission of energy and power, recite
the Medicine Buddha mantra 21 or 108 times:

TAYATA OM BHEKHANDZE BHEKHANDZE MAHA
BHEKHANDZE BHEKHANDZE RANDZA SAMUNGATE
SOHA

Now imagine that Medicine Buddha reduces in size directly above
our crown to the size of a mustard seed. He enters the crown of our
head and travels down the central channel to our heart. The Buddha dissolves into light and this light merges with our own body
and fills us with light, healing and power.

Dedication

May the heart of awakening which has not yet risen, arise now and
grow. May that which has arisen never diminish, but increase more
and more.

May the merit of this practice benefit all beings and may all beings be well and happy and free from suffering.

This completes the meditation.

NOTE: If one wishes to facilitate this meditation on behalf of another, one imagines the same process is occurring at the same time for the person concerned. We imagine the person we wish to heal to be sitting before us and that a Medicine Buddha is sitting above their head. Effectively, two streams of healing lights flow from the Buddha above our head and the Buddha above the recipients head.

Medicine Buddha and Absent Healing

Here we use guided imagery, the Medicine Buddha mantra, Reiki symbols and Absent Healing to assist in the healing process for oneself or another.

Procedure

1. Call the person requiring healing by stating their name three times, and accessing their mind stream with the Sei Heki. Once you feel a connection with the person, proceed with the following:
2. Draw: Honsha Ze Shonen, Sei Heki, Choku Rei.
3. Visualize Medicine Buddha above the recipient's head facing the same direction as them. Visualize white light emanating from Medicine Buddha pouring like rain and flowing into the body and mind of the recipient.
4. While this is occurring, recite the Medicine Buddha mantra 21 or 108 times.
5. Now visualize a blue energy emanating from Medicine Buddha, which pours like rain into the recipient, energizing and clearing physical obstructions.
6. While this is occurring, recite the Medicine Buddha mantra 21 or 108 times.
7. Once this is complete, visualize Medicine Buddha condensing in space and traveling through the recipient's central channel from the crown to the heart. Imagine Medicine Buddha dissolving into the heart of the recipient, filling them with healing power and light.
8. Share the merit of this healing practice and give thanks in your own way.
9. Once this feels complete, sign the Choku Rei and close in the usual manner.

NOTE: *This procedure can be extended by including the specific visualizations and details from the previous meditation on Medicine Buddha.*

Medicine Buddha and Hands-on Healing

The healing qualities of Medicine Buddha can be incorporated into your hands on session in a similar fashion to your absent healing. Imagine or visualize a small Medicine Buddha above the head of the individual you are treating. The Buddha is facing the same direction as the recipient. As you are facilitating Reiki healing, see the streams of light coming from the heart of Medicine Buddha down through the crown Chakra of the recipient and going to the affected areas, healing the obstructions that are causing illness and imbalance. As you are seeing this happen, all the while you are reciting the Mantra silently in your mind:

TAYATA OM BHEKHANDZE BHEKHANDZE MAHA BHEKHANDZE BHEKHANDZE RANDZA SAMUNGATE SOHA

Once you have finished the treatment, condense the Buddha into light and let it travel down the central channel where it resides in the heart of the recipient. Give thanks in your own way and finish in the usual manner.

In cases of serious illnesses do not dissolve the Medicine Buddha in the heart, rather see the Medicine Buddha continuing to radiate healing energy for the recipient.

This procedure can greatly increase the effectiveness of your sessions, while also receiving the blessing, the bestowal of healing and merit of Medicine Buddha.

The Importance of Direct Transmission

For one to fully engage in the practices of Medicine Buddha, one requires the appropriate initiations from a qualified Buddhist Lama. One also needs to take Refuge in the Buddhist teachings and receive the empowerments of the sacred texts concerning the practice. The form presented above acts as a starting point for all non-Buddhists and can be practiced by anyone who sincerely wishes to benefit all sentient beings with the healing power of Medicine Buddha.

These meditations can also be adapted to your specific needs. You may wish to visualize a fountain of light or an Angel or some other symbol that speaks to you. The symbolism we use is a tool to focus the mind on the practice.

Death and Dying

'You too will die some day,
knowing this, how can you quarrel?'

— THE BUDDHA

Assisting someone at the point of death can be a great gift for the person making their transition. Later in this chapter we will outline the methods that can assist an individual who has died but before we explain this process it is necessary to have a basic understanding of the dying process. The following section describes the key stages of the dying process and is inspired by the teachings described in *The Tibetan Book of the Dead*.

What happens when we die?

Most of our western views on death and dying are generally concerned with the lead up to ones departure from this world and there is little consideration or knowledge of the matter to the way one actually makes this transition. Usually if the person is a Christian, a priest is present to give the person confession and to say some prayers. Because many Western religious systems have no concept of the inner channels and the experience of dying, there is not a great deal of teachings one can rely on. Many of these religions rely heavily on faith and a belief in an outer God. As a result once the person has died it is largely a matter of hoping that the priest did a good job and that the dead one will be met by a kind and forgiving God. Essentially, the consideration of the internal workings of consciousness is largely left up to the Almighty.

From the Buddhist point of view there is a great deal of information regarding the stages that one goes through from this life to the next. Through the depth insight of enlightened practitioners of the Dharma, detailed information concerning this transition is practiced to help sentient beings through the Bardo.

In order to appreciate this view it is important to understand that our physical body is not our mind. We should recognize that we are in fact consciousness occupying a body. Our minds were never born and can never die. Our minds are timeless without beginning or end and from one life to the next we take rebirth again and again throughout cyclic existence. If you like, our mind or true essence is like space, and our body is a vehicle or container for our mind during each life.

When our physical body ceases to function, our mind becomes once again like space, so wherever we think, this is where we are.

For example, we think of our loved ones and we are before them or we think of our favorite place in nature and there we are. The mind has no container (the body), and therefore can be anywhere at will. We know this to be true in the ways our thoughts shape reality. For example, when we think of a friend and the next day we bump into them or when someone calls and we know who it is.

Recognizing that our minds are not our bodies and that we have many lives, we will now detail the stages leading up to the dying process.

The inner stages leading up to death and the stages that follow

From the Tibetan Buddhist perspective there are essentially two phases of dissolution for someone dying. These are the outer dissolution, where the five elements or sense impressions dissolve or cease to function and the inner dissolution, where the inner channels of thought and emotion dissolve.

Let us first look at the outer dissolution of a dying person. As human beings we are made up of five sense elements. These are Earth, Water, Fire, Air and Space, which is our true essence or 'Clear Light'.

In the moments leading up to one's death, the first of these senses to dissolve is the element of Earth. Here our body begins to lose all its strength. We are unable to hold ourselves upright, we begin to feel heavy and uncomfortable in any position and we may ask to be propped up with pillows or for others to help us in keeping upright and stable. During the dissolution of this element it becomes harder to keep our eyelids open and our mind becomes drowsy. This indicates the dissolution of the earth element.

The next element to cease functioning is the Water element. Here we lose control of our bodily fluids, our nose and eyes begin to run, and we may dribble or even become incontinent.

Following this, the element of Fire begins to dissolve. Here we become very thirsty and our body begins to become cool. All of our outer extremities become cold and lifeless and the warmth of our body begins to condense into the center of our body. Here our mind swings between clarity and confusion. We also find it hard to recognize loved ones as sight and sound are also confused. Our breath is cold as it passes through our mouth and nostrils and this leads us into the fourth element of Air.

As the Air element begins to dissolve, it becomes harder and harder to breathe. Our in-breaths become more and more shallow and our out-breaths become longer and longer. Our minds become a blur with no recognition of the outside world. Lastly we breathe out three long breaths and do not breathe in again. All of our vital signs are gone and for all intents and purposes we are dead. Although this is when most loved ones pack to go home, from the Tibetan view, this is the beginning of the inner dissolution.

The dissolution of the inner winds

From the Buddhist perspective, the dissolution of the inner winds takes anywhere from twenty to thirty minutes. The procedure that follows later in this chapter can be of particular benefit during this time, but more on this later.

It is during this time that the internal energies of the body collect in the central energy channel. It is at this point that the white essence that resides at the crown Chakra begins to travel through the central channel from the crown to the heart center. This process takes approximately ten to fifteen minutes. This White energy represents the Male or Sperm of the Father Essence. It is during this time that thirty-three emotions related to anger are liberated.

Once this White energy reaches the heart center, there is a tremendous light that is beyond words in power and beauty. The ecstatic sensation represents the liberation of the negative emotions relating to anger from the lifetime.

At this point, it is worth noting that in most research and case studies concerning N.D.E.s (near death experience), we find a common element here. Often with N.D.E., the common experience is of traveling through a white tunnel going to a tremendous light. Those who have come back to tell their tale describe the joy and renewed respect for life which comes from such an experience. This experience is suggestive of the white essence traveling down the central channel. And the tremendous joy experienced is the liberation of negative emotions as our consciousness journeys' along the central channel.

What follows next is the Red energy, representing the Female or Egg of the Mother essence. This essence now begins to journey upwards through the central channel. This Red essence resides in the navel, four finger-widths below the belly button in the center of the body. This essence journeys up through the central channel towards the heart center. This process also takes anywhere from ten to fifteen minutes and it is during this time that forty emotions relating to attachment are liberated. Once these two internal energies meet at the heart center, mind is like deep space. In this moment, seven emotions relating to Ignorance are liberated and with this there is an incredible light that is so overwhelming that the mind of the person simply loses consciousness. This light is the true essence or true nature of our mind. Unless we are experienced meditators and can recognize this light as our own minds the person loses consciousness for a period of anywhere between sixty-eight to seventy-two hours.

It is after this time that the mind of the person begins to wake up. Often the mind of the dead one is confused from the experience and tries to communicate with friends and loved ones from the former life.

In the mind of the dead one, they perceive themselves as having a physical form. This is because the mind of the dead one is still strongly attached to their conditioned impressions from their former life.

Because he mind has no container yet it thinks it is still physical, the mind of the dead one will try to communicate with the living and receive no response. One will walk across fine sand and leave no prints. One will look into mirrors and see no reflection and eventually it dawns on the being that they are in fact dead. The shock of this realization will often be so distressing that the mind of the person will once again black out. This experience is the intermediary state called 'the Bardo'.

It is during this period that experiences of friends or dear ones of the departed may sense that they can feel the deceased nearby, or that they are having a conversation with them. It is with these experiences that the being is making some contact on a psychic/telepathic connection to one's relatives or loved ones. Many people put this down to their imagination, but it is usually the case that contact is actually being made.

This transitory state takes approximately seven days from the time of regaining consciousness. During the next seven days the strong subconscious impressions begin to surface. One will stay in these impressions until one has served out the necessary karma and then these impressions finally dissolve. This can last anywhere from a few hours or days and up to a total of forty-nine days from the persons' death. At this time a clear light comes and the being makes their transition from this Bardo to their next rebirth.

In the transition to their next rebirth, one will see their future parents. Pulled by the Laws of Karma, the mind will go to the future parents, entering the male through the crown Chakra during lovemaking. The consciousness is then born as the White male essence and Red female essence unites (sperm and egg in fertilization).

It is from here the being begins their next life and so it goes.

The Blessing of the Pure Realm, Dewachen

Now that we have looked at the various stages of death and rebirth, we will look at how we can assist a person during this process.

The following procedure can assist a person through these Bardos so that they can go directly to a pure realm (Dewachen) and achieve a favorable rebirth. To assist one in this process, one needs to facilitate this under the following conditions:

BUDDHA AMITABHA

- Between the point of death and the following thirty minutes.

- Between the third day to the forty ninth day of the person dying by sending the healing every seven days on the anniversary of the persons' death.

- This process can be facilitated either in the location of the deceased or as an absent healing procedure.

- This process can be continued until the seventh week or until there is no presence of the being at the calling in stage. (Stage 1 in the procedure that follows.)

Procedure to assist a being's transition through dying

1. Call the person in three times using the Absent Healing procedure. If you are present with the individual, call in the mind in the same way. Once you have a clear sign that the mind of the individual is present, state briefly your intentions and what you will be doing for them. Remember, they have a psychic link to your mind at this point and know your thoughts, so this can either be said out loud or silently.

2. Sign the three symbols to bridge the Reiki energy to the one who has died: Honsha Ze Shonen, Sei Heki, Choku Rei.

3. Set your intention that there is a Red Buddha (Amitabha) above the head of the individual facing the same direction as them.

4. Now visualize the person going into the heart of this Red Buddha through the crown of their head and up through the body of Buddha Amitabha.

5. As you are visualizing this happening recite the Mantra 108 times, seeing them going into the heart of Amitabha Buddha. Recite: 'Om Ami Dewa Hrih'.

6. Recite three times the offering prayer: *'Buddha Amitabha, please bestow your blessings on 'state the persons name', and grant him/her the freedom from the attachment to this life. Granting them the blessing of your pure realm, Dewachen.'*

7. Repeat the visualization and mantras again or until you sense their movement from this world to the realm of Dewachen.

8. Once this feels complete, give thanks in your own way and dedicate the merit of this practice for the benefit of all sentient beings.

9. Complete the healing by signing the Choku Rei and blow through your cupped hands three times.

NOTE: One should repeat this process on the seventh day, each week following their death. Once you feel that no connection can be made in the 'calling in' stage, this is a clear sign they have moved completely from this realm.

It should be noted that this procedure is a simplified form of 'Phowa' and does not confer the complete instructions. The method present here is an introduction to the concepts of assisting beings in their transition, and to confer a blessing and assistance in this process. It is highly recommended for one to accomplish a greater understanding of this process, that one completes a Phowa retreat, (conscious dying), with a qualified Lama as well as receiving Buddhist refuge and the initiation for Amitabha in the form of Wonkur (initiation).

For further reading on this subject and a deeper explanation of these concepts please refer to *The Tibetan Book of Living and Dying* by Sogyal Rinpoche. For details of Phowa retreats worldwide visit: www.diamondway.org

Bringing it All Together

At this level the practitioner has worked with a large variety of ways of using the universal energy of Reiki. In one's Reiki practice, it is essential to consider each person that you treat in a new light each time. One can easily get into a routine of facilitating a Reiki session and doing the same techniques without consideration to the individual and their particular needs. This is fine if you are simply facilitating a basic Reiki First Degree hands on treatment, the energy will work on a general level for that being's highest good.

If, however, you are working with specific methods for directing universal energy, i.e., directing symbols, Medicine Buddha, etc., your personal awareness, being centered and holding focus become vital factors in directing the Reiki energy in these specific ways.

To the best of our ability, our mind should be pure, with the aspiration of being a clear channel for the healing of Medicine Buddha and for this healing energy to be passed through ourselves and into the recipient. Treat your session much like a meditation, be watchful of your thoughts and watch your mind. If you feel yourself thinking about the weekend or what you are going to be doing later, then you are not there for the person, so bring yourself back and be mindful.

When we are present we are in flow in Body, Speech and Mind, and out of this comes the essence of being one with Reiki. It is good advice to cultivate this in your personal self-healing and in the treatment of others.

CHAPTER SIXTEEN

'When you come to a fork in the road, take it.'

— YOGI BERRA

Reiki Third Degree — Level 3A

In this chapter we will illustrate some of the basic methods of the Third Degree level. As one might appreciate, not all of the Third Degree methods are presented here, as these methods require a readiness on behalf of the student and initiation into the third degree. It is also important that one should only attempt to use the methods presented within this level, corresponding to your own level of Reiki initiation.

When it comes to the traditional Third Degree in Reiki the levels are often split into two sections. (Note: traditions vary in this approach). These are the A and B sides. The A side represents the Third Degree Practitioners Level and the B side represents Teacher Training.

Although one can learn level 3A and work with the Reiki energy of the Third Degree, the A side does not qualify oneself as a Reiki teacher. The 3A level simply gives the methods of attunement, some advanced healing practices as well as the Third Degree Symbol.

Teacher training or what could be referred to as Reiki Masters Training requires an additional initiation and further procedures. This will be outlined in the following chapter.

The benefits of learning Reiki 3A are many. The following is an overview of what is covered during the training.

1. Participants receive the Reiki 3A attunement. This attunement increases the power and an ability to facilitate healing on much broader and expansive levels.

2. Participants receive the Reiki Third Degree Symbol. This is the fourth symbol in the Reiki system. This symbol is used in the

Reiki initiation procedures, which are taught to create a powerful alignment with the Reiki energy.

3. Participants learn a variety of advanced methods for local and distant healing, including distant attunements, self-attunements, group attunements, healing locations, hands on initiation procedures, and duplicating initiations. Participants also learn the theory and practice of initiations, what they are and the keys to how they work.

4. In 3A, two initiations are imparted:

A. The first attunement of First Degree Reiki. This attunement can be given to anyone and will give a temporary alignment to the Reiki energy. With this one can be shown the Reiki hand positions and the recipient can begin to utilize the healing energies. This initiation can also be given to someone who already has Reiki to enhance his or her Reiki ability.

B. The Reiki II Booster Initiation. This attunement can be given to practitioners who have already been attuned to the Second Degree or higher, to increase their healing ability and energy. It also may be sent over a distance to people or places and into the past or future.

The Reiki 3A Attunement

The 3A initiation works on opening the inner ear and the divine eye and as a result this attunement enhances the capacities of ones' intuition, perception and clairvoyance.

The First Degree Temporary Alignment

This alignment gives the recipient the ability to empower themselves through hands on healing. This has proved most successful in clinical work, where the client comes for healing and wishes to continue their practice between sessions. This simple procedure transfers the Reiki energy, creating an alignment for the individual, so that they are taking an active role in their own healing process. It should be noted that this alignment has a temporary effect. The attunement lasts anywhere from three weeks to three months and these times vary from individual to individual.

Self-attunement Procedures

When bestowing self-attunements there are three methods. These are as follows:

Method 1. Physically drawing the Reiki attunement procedure on oneself.

Here the student learns how to facilitate an attunement procedure on oneself. This is a valuable exercise to promote and activate the universal life force energy in daily life.

Giving self-attunements also boosts the immune system and acts as a means of purification and protection from negative influences.

Method 2. Completely visualizing the procedure.

This method is the same as the previous one, however it varies in the approach. Here the student uses creative visualization. There are a number of variations on this method, such as self-arising, front arising, third person and duplication methods.

Method 3. Visualization and the use of Mudras as symbolic memory cues.

Here the student combines the two previous methods with a great emphasis on visualization. The method incorporates the use of Mudra (hand gestures) to determine where one is in the initiation procedure. These Mudras also summon power and particular frequencies of the Reiki energy and symbols. With practice, Mudras alone can generate the power of the initiations.

Absent Initiations

Sending an Absent initiation is a great solution when a person due to locality cannot be present to learn Reiki. The very notion that we can send Absent Healing makes Absent initiations only a step up to directing the Reiki Energy.

The procedure for sending an Absent initiation follows a similar path to Absent healing. The person requesting the attunement is 'called in' and their mind stream is transferred to a proxy of your choice. One then simply performs the initiation procedure, either physically as if the individual were present, or by visualizing the procedure, using the law of correspondence to direct the attunement to the specific points of the energy system. One can also use one's own body as a proxy by performing a self-attunement procedure, corresponding this alignment to another. This way, both the recipient and the practitioner receive the initiation.

Another variation to this procedure is to have a photo of the person and to place this on a chair. Once the person has been called in, using the standard procedure, one performs the initiation process as if it were a person seated before them. One imagines a form of energy and light and facilitates the procedure just as if a real person were present.

With all these approaches, it is important to close the procedure in a standard fashion as with all Absent Healing procedures.

Absent initiations can be particularly beneficial in assisting others during times when there is a great deal of negativity or suffering present within an individual. This is also the case for particular locations or places that have been subject to negative impressions. Sending Absent initiations is a very powerful way to direct the healing power of Reiki to assist in the removal of negative forces and to aid in the best possible outcome of situations. In this way the initiations align the individual, location, or object with the Reiki energy.

Group Initiations

Aside from individual initiations, a number of students may initiate one individual at a time. This squares the energy, much like group hands on healing. This method generates a greater amount of Universal energy filling the individual at one time. This has numerous effects for the recipient and can be used to remove strong blockages, obstacles, serious illnesses and negative patterns in the mind of the person receiving.

The Third Degree Reiki Symbol
The Great Light: Dai Koumyo

The Dai Koumyo is one of the central pillars of the Reiki system. Once a teacher has received the necessary empowerment for this Reiki symbol, which is usually given at the Third Degree, the teacher then learns its function and the methodology by which to bestow Reiki attunements upon others.

The following is a brief outline of the symbols meaning and uses at this level:

DAI: Great, big; huge; magnificent expansion; all-pervading.

KOO: Light radiating in all directions; fine light; radiance; expansion at crown Chakra.

MYO: Too clear to doubt; clairvoyance; moonlight shining through the window; the divine light illuminating the darkness of ignorance; the merging of the sun and moon; forming a great light; the Enlightened One (the light of Buddha's wisdom, expansive all permeating light, radiating from the head (halo) of the enlightened one).

DAI KOUMYO Uses*:

• Dai Koumyo activates all the Chakras and energy channels.
• Dai Koumyo affects the three Spiritual Centers above the Heart:

Crown, 3rd Eye and the Throat Chakras.

• It activates the union of Universal energy and the individuals energy system, creating the alignment with the Reiki energy.

• Calls in the Universal energy that dispels negativity and clears the veils of ignorance that block the minds true nature.

• It summons healing and spiritual forces that oversee the Reiki system.

* NOTE: The information presented does not detail the inner, secret meaning of this symbol, nor the method for bestowing Reiki attunement. These methods can only be given to a teacher under supervised training within this tradition.

As with the symbols of the Second Degree there is a strong emphasis on signing the Reiki Symbols correctly and with full awareness. This is especially beneficial training for the mind when it comes time to learn the Reiki initiations. At this level, one requires concentration, an ability to be still and to be able to hold focus on the task at hand. It is a great responsibility to attune another to Reiki, so we need our full awareness and mental focus out of respect for the individual receiving this alignment. This is also important so that we perform the attunements correctly.

Reiki Initiation, A Pathway to the Removal of Obstacles

Each time we facilitate an initiation for either ourselves or another, we clear more and more of the veils that prevent our true nature. Much like the analogy of the sun on a cloudy day. The sun represents our Buddha nature whole and awakened. The clouds represent our negative conditioning, our ignorance, and our accumulated negative actions that we have formed in former lives.

We all know the sun is there, but when the clouds are present, our view is obscured, preventing us from knowing ourselves as being whole.

When we facilitate an initiation procedure, we are calling forth a tremendous amount of universal energy with the Dai Koumyo. Each attunement procedure actively clears more of these clouds, thereby transforming ourselves in the process.

The initiation procedures are a great way to clear ourselves on a daily level. The practice of self-attunements, or where possible, group attunements, gives the practitioner the opportunity to refine their abilities of concentration and focus. These attunements also have a wonderful purification effect upon the practitioner and are a way to clear many things within our being.

Some practitioners facilitate the self-attunement procedures on a daily level, sometimes doing numerous attunements each day when working on specific issues.

One may say that one only needs to be attuned to the Reiki energy once, much like a doorway that has been unlocked. This is certainly true; however, the repetition of this practice clears the inner channels and energetic system of the body and subsequently has a direct effect on whatever requires healing or clearing within the body.

CHAPTER SEVENTEEN

*'The most beautiful experience we can have is the mysterious. It
is the fundamental emotion, which stands at the cradle of true
art and science. Whoever does not know it and can no longer
marvel, is as good as dead, and his eyes are dimmed.'*

— ALBERT EINSTEIN

Reiki 3B Teacher Training Program

The call, the decision to become a Reiki teacher

To become a Reiki teacher is a further step in one's path of service
to humanity. Being a teacher of Reiki is not for everyone as it requires a deep commitment to healing oneself and others. Many
people these days learn the Reiki teacher level, yet never intend to
teach.

If you like, to become a teacher and to pass on the Reiki system
is much like receiving the 'call'. This is indeed a great honor and a
privilege and should be considered carefully.

To be a Reiki teacher is to be a holder of the light. What this
means is to be one who carries the Reiki lineage and the power of
the Universal Energy to others. So it can be seen as a great responsibility to pass on this tradition and even more importantly, with
integrity and honor.

Reiki is a path of healing but more than that it is a path of awakening. The more we actively embrace and live the practice, the
more our awakening and potential as human beings unfolds. This
is Reiki as it should be.

So, responding to this call is not a matter of waking up one day
and saying: 'I wonder what I'll do today. Oh, I'll become a Reiki
teacher.' The call comes from a place deep within, it can certainly
be activated by an experience in our lives, a chance meeting, an
illness or relationship; it can simply be an inner knowing. Whichever way the 'call' comes, the decision to be a holder of the Reiki

tradition is a wonderful thing to do.

In making the decision to become a teacher we need to consider our motivation very carefully; status, position and money should be at the bottom of your list of reasons to take this step. Candidates for teacher training are accepted with respect to their level of understanding, practice and integration, spiritual potential, personal motivation and level of integrity. The path of being a Reiki teacher is not necessarily an easy path, for it requires one to be a living example of Reiki and this means one needs to embody the practices and live Reiki to the best of our ability.

The following is an outline of the teacher's path and briefly what it takes to become a teacher.

Reiki 3B. Teacher training is for those individuals who feel drawn to pass on the Reiki System. 3B takes the form of an apprenticeship and empowers the ability to permanently initiate and attune people to Reiki levels I and II. Participants learn workshop presentation and facilitation, initiation and attunement procedures.

The apprenticeship includes: co-teaching and participating in Reiki I and II workshops, coordination of Healing Clinics and related community service projects.

In addition to this, participants learn workshop presentation, personal development skills, group dynamics and other related spiritual disciplines, which unfold throughout the training.

Participants also receive the 3B Initiation. This initiation empowers the person to teach Reiki levels First and Second degree.

The time duration for apprenticing varies from individual to individual. The training time is anywhere from nine months to two years.

The prerequisite to attending the training program is a completion of the Reiki I, II, and Reiki 3A levels. A candidate of this level requires a direct lineage in the Reiki system and preferably, one should have received these initiations in sequence with the same Reiki teacher. This is to maintain consistency with initiation procedures, as there are many variations of these procedures from teacher to teacher.

Applicants are also required to submit a personal assessment life mapping questionnaire and an essay on why they wish to become a teacher of Reiki.

At the completion of the apprenticeship, the teacher in training participates in a training module to integrate the methods taught. At this point, final initiations are bestowed and the teacher is empowered to initiate students of their own in Reiki. A new teacher may also continue to participate in workshops with the Senior

Reiki Instructor to fine tune initiations and gain direct experience of being a teacher of Reiki.

Once a student has completed their training, they also receive a certificate in Reiki 3B and are granted the title 'Reiki Instructor or Sensei' under the guidelines of the IIRT.

What is a Reiki Master?

Put simply, a Reiki Master is a teacher of Reiki. In the west there seems to be some confusion surrounding this word. For many this term equates in peoples minds as a grey haired Guru who has special spiritual abilities. However, when we look at what it means to 'master' something, it makes sense that one has a certain level of accomplishment in ones art. If we think of a Master craftsman, we think of someone who has spent years, and in most cases decades refining their training and skill and someone who has the experience of their trade to back this kind of title.

So when it comes to Reiki and Mastering Reiki, this is something that one would consider in a similar way. The Third degree or Masters Reiki is a level for those who want to be teachers of the system.

When Reiki made its way to America in the early 1970's, the term for teacher was replaced in the west with the term Reiki Master.

Unfortunately for Reiki today one can simply participate in a seminar for the third degree and at the end of as little as one or two days can have a certificate staying that one is a 'Master of Reiki'. One can even buy this title over the Internet! (Provided you have paid enough money.)

Reiki Mastery is not something that should be bought, but something that comes through years of dedicated practice. Even then, a teacher of humble disposition would shy away from calling themselves a Master of Reiki.

The term 'Master' is usually given out of respect to a teacher by their students. And in light of this information, someone who has completed the third degree and is a teacher of that system would be better served by being called a 'Teacher, Instructor or Sensei' of Reiki.

The ultimate goal of any spiritual practice is to gain liberation from suffering and to benefit others in this goal. Self-elation and inflating ones Ego with grand titles can be a real obstacle on the path and one needs to keep in check with this. Even better to have genuine friends or a spiritual teacher who has the kindness to burst your Ego's bubble when you need it.

The term 'Reiki Master' was never actually used in Japan. We see today so many people pumping themselves up with titles to make themselves and their egos feel important.

There's a saying that goes: 'Anyone who says they are enlightened, isn't.'

One demonstrates their accomplishment through their actions of kindness and compassion.

It is through living Reiki that we let our light shine for others to see. It would be foolish for ourselves to talk about how spiritual we are if we have not mastered our own minds. Therefore, it is essential to walk this path with deep respect and humility for the vast nature of mind.

The following teaching says this well: *"The foolish who know themselves as fools have at least some wisdom. For fools who think themselves as wise are truly foolish"*. – *Verse 63, The Dhammapada*.

His Holiness the Dalai Lama puts this beautifully when he says that he is 'just a simple Buddhist monk'. One should never put oneself above another or be beyond the basic tasks of life. The path of humility is an important path for a teacher of Reiki, it is a virtue that is learned with time. This is always why we give thanks for our lives and dedicate our newfound wisdom for the benefit of others.

How long does it take to become a Reiki teacher?

The period of time for one to become an authorized teacher will vary greatly depending upon the teachings offered, the teacher offering the teachings and the teacher in training.

As a general guide Dr. Usui prescribed a minimum of two years practice with the first and second degrees, before his students were invited to participate in the Third degree. Of those who were deemed ready, willing, and more importantly able to teach, they were then invited to continue under a probationary period or until they were deemed competent to teach their own students. In some cases this was over several years, though Dr. Usui usually authorized a student after one to two years of dedicated teacher training.

One should also think in terms of realistic goals. If for example I was learning a martial Art, such as Tae-Kwon-Do, I could learn for many years and still not have a sound foundation and ability to instruct others in the finer points of this art. Just because one learns Reiki, does not mean one has an ability to pass it on. One not only needs a solid foundation of the methods and techniques, one must have embodied the inner experience. This is achieved through hundreds of treatments and regular self-application. How else can one have a suitable source to draw upon when instructing others? If one thinks that by participating in a weekend workshop one will 'get it all', then one would be better served with a broader view.

The Seminars

As part of the on-going mentorship and training, the Reiki Seminars are an excellent training ground for teachers in training. A teacher-in-training may participate in several seminars as part of their apprenticeship. The teacher-in-training's role is to take personal notes on the procedures, to ask questions and to simply observe. One's ability to observe is an important part of becoming a teacher. It is through this method that one comes to learn the subtle group energies unfolding during a workshop.

After a teacher-in-training has a solid understanding of the techniques taught there is then the opportunity to teach parts of the workshop and eventually co-teach with the senior instructor.

Usually after assisting in a number of Reiki workshops, the teacher in training is given the empowerment for Reiki 3B. The initiation procedures are then taught for the four Reiki I empowerments and the Reiki II empowerment. The teacher-in-training may also be asked to participate in an additional two workshops after their 3B training module to assist the senior teacher in the initiation procedures of Reiki levels, First and Second degree.

It is suggested that new Reiki teachers facilitate at least four Reiki I workshops before they facilitate a Reiki II workshop, or to wait at least a period of six months. The reasons for this are simple. It allows time to integrate the initiations of Reiki I. The new teacher needs this time to integrate, and this also allows the Reiki I students time before moving them to the second degree. Meanwhile, running other workshops and initiating others in first degree allows the teacher time to adjust to the higher frequencies running through his/her body as it takes time to adjust to this level of the Reiki energy.

Self Mastery

It is surprising how many people develop a concept of being spiritual. This can be a trap of sorts and a way of replacing one set of neuroses with another. A common experience with personal growth is the misconceptions of the ego mind. As we move along the spiritual path, we naturally want to hold onto the happy and pleasurable experiences and wish to move away from anything negative. Only focusing on our positive self is one part of the whole, in order to grow in a honest way we also need to come to terms with and face our shadow self. Self-acceptance is not about a single pointed idealistic view of ourselves. It is far better to accept ourselves from where we are. When we experience pain or discomfort in our lives, our immediate response is to remove this discomfort and to change our current dilemma to a more favorable situation. There are certainly many times when this is most appropriate; however, in facing and examining our response and even allowing ourselves to be still in that reaction can be a tremendous learning vehicle.

The philosophy of being able to be still in the face of adversity and to move into that experience reveals much about our conditioning. Therefore when someone presses your buttons either through careless words or actions, instead of reacting to this, try to identify the cause of the reaction. People are our mirrors, be watchful and you will begin to see yourself. A teacher needs to be a mirror and needs to know oneself. This takes time and learning. If you are the kind of person who has some unresolved issues to do with your sexuality, anger, abandonment, control, sensuality, dependency or other emotional issues, then one should face these conditioned views and do ones best to heal these issues. There is no shame in seeing a good therapist, even good therapists see their own therapist. Take a moment to list your current issues, be honest with yourself, this is the first step to becoming more authentic.

The following are some points to consider:

1. Ask for others' feedback in your teaching abilities and how you interact with others.
2. Look at your response when others give you criticism.
3. Keep a journal of your positive responses to Reiki and look at your personal motive for being a teacher.
4. Be prepared to look at your shadow issues and seek outside guidance when needed.
5. Dedicate, daily, all your actions, abilities, belongings, your body and mind for the benefit of all that lives.
6. Donate a part of your earnings to a worthy cause, give donations to charities, offer service to others and give some of your time away without the expectation of return.
7. Write a list of your short-comings, now compare these with your personal attributes.
8. Daily, offer prayers that all beings be well and happy and free

from harm.

9. Surrender to the movement of spirit in your life. Let go, let spirit guide you, but remember to get off your behind and meet spirit half way!

10. Have purpose to your day, live each day dedicated to love, service, and compassion.

Teacher Training Requirements

The following is the Institutes 3B Teacher Training application. This is designed to map out the commitments required and personal self-evaluation necessary before beginning the training. This self-assessment process is an interesting process as it is designed to take the applicant into a deeper relationship with their motivations and aspirations for becoming a teacher of Reiki.

The Reiki Teachers Training program is an apprenticeship offered by the International Institute for Reiki Training. In undertaking such a commitment there are a number of requirements to be satisfied.

The following endeavors to highlight these requirements and what it means to embark on the path of Reiki Teachers Training.

The commitments of this path are broken down into three parts:

1. Your first commitment is to the movement of Spirit in your life, the Universal energy and the way in which this energy shapes your life.

2. Your second commitment is to your own healing process and the pursuit of the path of healing others.

3. Your third commitment is to the Reiki Lineage, the teachings and the teachers of the tradition.

As you begin this journey you will find the universal energy will shape you and your life. It is like a preparation for becoming a fit vessel for universal energy. This often includes purification and opportunities to heal our personal agendas.

As we deepen our commitment to the Reiki path we begin to recognize the inner qualities. The result of being in the energy and especially in having the responsibility of teaching and attuning others brings with it many gifts. We become closer to the source of our own becoming. There is a deep understanding of peace, awareness and our interconnectedness to all that lives. Becoming a teacher does not mean that you will become a spiritual being, it is more like you are shown the door to become this. The stepping through is the practice, dedication and union with the teachings.

As seekers of the path, we need to recognize our foibles and take the challenge to move beyond these to something far greater.

The IIRT Teachers Code

As teachers of Reiki we should endeavor to honor the teachers code.

1. All Reiki Instructors acknowledge, honor and respect Mikao Usui as the founding father of Reiki.
2. All Reiki Instructors acknowledge all other legitimate Reiki schools and teachers, regardless of personal differences and beliefs.
3. All Reiki Instructors agree to a uniform and consistent approach with regard to initiation, methodology and practice.
4. All Reiki Instructors strive for personal and professional excellence as representatives of the standards and ethics of Reiki in practice.

Prerequisites for 3B

1. A sincere desire to serve humanity in the pursuit of healing.
2. Your preparedness to support and to be available for your initiating teacher and your fellow students.
3. Your willingness to understand, integrate and learn the material in the training program.
4. A willingness to learn in a grounded, practical and realistic manner.
5. The completion and submission of your personal life mapping assessment questionnaire.
6. The completion and submission of your essay of personal motivation for teachers training.
7. The completion of the necessary Reiki training levels.
8. A personal commitment to upholding the standards and ethics held by the IIRT.
9. An acceptance and application of the IIRT Teachers training code.
10. The completion and submission of the application for IIRT teachers training.

Progressive training prior to completion of Reiki 3B

• Participating and co-teaching in Reiki workshops.
• The ability to organize, coordinate and promote Reiki workshops, clinics and related events.

- Showing an active interest in participating in Reiki clinics, support groups, personal healing, personal practice and other related projects.
- A willingness to donate time and energy to service those in need and to community based services.
- Serving an apprenticeship with the initiating Reiki Instructor.

Personal Life Mapping Assessment

QUESTIONNAIRE

The following is the teacher training application and personal life assessment. (Parts A and B are submitted prior to the commencement of the training.)

Part A

Answer these questions as best as you can. This is an exercise for you.

1. In the past, what have I realized in the areas of...
   - Family?
   - Work?
   - Friendships?
   - Relationships?
   - Spiritual Path?
   - My Shadow?
   - Personal Growth?

2. What have I wanted but never had in these areas?

3. What brings me out of harmony in relation to...
   A. My path?
   B. Myself?

4. What are my greatest fears in relation to....
   A. My path?
   B. Myself?

5. What roles do I play in my life? Which of these serve my path?

6. What do I need to do right now to further my journey along my path?

7. What are my strengths? What are my weaknesses?

8. What is my definition of myself as a teacher of Reiki?

9. What is my Spiritual path and how can I nurture this?

Part B

Essay: (approximately 1,000 words).

Write as honestly and authentically as you can:

'Why do I want to become a Reiki teacher and what does this mean to me?'

CHAPTER EIGHTEEN

'Miracles, wonders, clairvoyance, clairaudience –
what are these? The greatest miracle is to realize the Self.
All these are side-tracks. The realized person is above them.'

— SRI RAMANA MAHARSHI

Advanced Teacher Training

Senior Reiki Instructor

A teacher who has completed their teacher training and who has been upholding the Reiki tradition by teaching Reiki levels First and Second Degree can be said to be an Instructor of Reiki. When a teacher decides to teach one of their own students the teachers level, then one is said to be a Senior Reiki Instructor.

Some Reiki styles have an additional attunement for this level, granting the teacher the ability to attune and empower their own students to teach Reiki. Although time requirements differ from one teacher to the next, this level of initiation is usually only offered after an instructor has been actively teaching for a minimum period of two years. These time requirements make sense, for if a teacher has not had adequate experience in teaching, how can they instruct others in this? So a teacher requires a solid experience in teaching to have the authority to teach a teacher.

The following is a general outline of training for the Senior Reiki Instructor Level.

This level of teacher's training empowers the teacher to initiate and train their own students to be teachers. This enables their student/teacher in training to teach the first and second levels of the Reiki System.

A teacher who has completed the Senior Instructor Level is empowered to teach Reiki levels: I, II, 3A, and 3B training programs and seminars.

During this training, which is often served as an apprenticeship, the teacher in training learns the initiation procedures for the higher levels as well as a variety of personal and spiritual practices. Upon successful completion of the training with the initiating Senior Reiki Instructor, the Reiki Instructor is then empowered to teach teachers and is granted the title 'Senior Reiki Instructor'.

Although many teachers of Reiki make no distinction between these teaching stages, some systems do. This level is also sometimes referred to as Reiki Fourth Degree.

The following is an outline of the overall training programs:

First Degree Reiki	Beginners
Second Degree Reiki	Intermediate
Third Degree Reiki (A)	Advanced Practitioner
Third Degree Reiki (B)	Teacher, Sensei, or Instructor
Fourth Degree Reiki	Senior Reiki Instructor

About the International Institute for Reiki Training (IIRT)

The International Institute for Reiki Training was born out of the wish to preserve and maintain a professional standard in the teaching and practice of Reiki. The IIRT's aim is to offer Reiki training by accredited facilitators who are of a professional standard. Equally, IIRT Reiki practitioners are trained with the aim of providing Reiki treatments that are of a genuine quality and service to the prospective client.

Another aim of the Institute is to offer Reiki to the wider community in the form of not for profit community services projects, like Reiki Healing Clinics.

The IIRT strives to present training that is educational, practical and innovative. The training also aims to hold true to the historical tradition, ethics and practice of the traditional Reiki system.

The IIRT Mission Statement

The International Institute for Reiki Training is dedicated to the pursuit of healing, education and personal/spiritual development for individuals and the community. Through teaching and healing others in a supportive and professional way the Institute seeks to maintain integrity in the teaching of traditional Reiki.

The IIRT Code of Ethics

1. IIRT practitioners shall conduct themselves in a professional and ethical manner, perform only those services for which they are

qualified, and represent their education, certification, professional affiliations and other qualifications honestly. IIRT practitioners do not in any way profess to practice medicine, psychotherapy or related practices, unless licensed to do so.

2. IIRT practitioners shall maintain clear and honest communications with their clients, and keep all client information, whether medical or personal, strictly confidential.

3. IIRT practitioners shall discuss any problem areas that may contravene the use of Reiki, and refer clients to appropriate medical or psychological professionals when indicated.

4. IIRT practitioners shall respect the client's physical/emotional state, and shall not abuse clients through actions, words or silence, nor take advantage of the therapeutic relationship. IIRT practitioners shall in no way participate in sexual activity with a client. They consider the client's comfort zone for touch and for degree of pressure, and honor the client's requests as much as possible within personal, professional and ethical limits. They acknowledge the inherent worth and individuality of each person and therefore do not unjustly discriminate against clients and fellow Reiki practitioners.

5. IIRT practitioners shall refrain from the abuse of alcohol and drugs. These substances should not be used at all during professional activities.

6. IIRT practitioners shall strive for professional excellence through regular assessment, personal development and by continued education and training.

7. Equality is practiced with all IIRT practitioners, regardless of which level, (including teachers/instructors), within the institute and related projects.

8. IIRT shall honor all other recognized and legitimate Reiki systems, practitioners and teachers regardless of personal differences and beliefs.

9. IIRT practitioners shall refrain from making false claims regarding potential benefits of Traditional Reiki.

10. IIRT practitioners shall in no way endeavor, either by personal act, word or deed to bring the IIRT or its teachers and tradition into disrepute.

In addition to the Institutes Code of Ethics, the IIRT also strives to abide by the following spiritual precepts.

The Ten Aspirations of Mindfulness

The following aspirations are Universal teachings for contemplation. These Dharmas* should not be considered commandments, nor should they be viewed as rules to obey. The emphasis of these aspirations is to present views that may inspire and support the practitioner. Each aspiration should be contemplated and then reviewed with personal attention and direct application to one's own life.

   * *Dharma. The word Dharma is derived from the Sanskrit language and refers to the teachings, which express universal laws or truth. Dharma is the teachings or laws, which uphold and support life and denotes the 'ways' to wisdom, liberation and peace.*

1. The Dharma of the Path

I hold the aspiration for the Path of Peace.

In all my actions, may I conduct myself in a manner which supports the path of unfolding. Through my practice may I be a light unto myself and cultivate self-reliance, unconditional love and compassion. May I recognize my ability to change and the freedom which comes by skillfully walking in the light of truth. May I know this way, never forget, nor stray. May this path be a path for many, may this be a path of love.

2. The Dharma of Tradition

I hold the aspiration to honor Tradition.

May I honor my teachers, elders, my spiritual lineage and all beings that have walked the path of peace. May I recognize the accumulated merit of this tradition and respectfully embrace the Dharma, these teachings and all who teach it. May my motivation be pure and may I hold the sacred traditions with deep respect, following the path of sages.

3. The Dharma of Right Speech.

I hold the aspiration to train myself in Right Speech.

I recognize the value of being sincere and honest in my words and use my speech to benefit others and myself. May I consider the effects of speech and diligently practice to refrain from mistruths, harsh or disturbing words and refrain from gossip or mindless opinions. Instead, may I have the courage to speak to those concerned and generate positive interactions. Throughout my days, may I aspire to be mindful of my internal speech, and steadfastly awaken speech that reflects and nurtures the heart of unfolding.

4. The Dharma of Generosity

I hold the aspiration to train myself in acts of Generosity.

I recognize the value of giving and receiving with right intent and serving others selflessly without desire for recognition or return. Through acts of service, may I generate a humble disposition. May I train myself to take only that which is freely given and to be mindful of the differences between wants, desires and needs. May I surrender my sectarian views and be ever watchful of pride, selfish actions and egotism. I take refuge in acts of service and steadfastly walk the path of Generosity.

5. The Dharma of Healing

I hold the aspiration to train myself in acts of healing.

May I recognize the precious opportunity in this life to know my body, speech and mind are tools for healing others and myself. I seek to know and use my healing abilities to assist humanity and to walk the healing path with humility, knowing my actions bear results. May I honor myself as a vehicle for Universal Energy and continue to consciously walk the path of healing for the benefit of all that lives.

6. The Dharma of Ecology

I hold the aspiration to recognize the interconnectedness of all existence.

May I practice mindfulness within my environment and value how my environment affects my body and mind. May I reverently appreciate and support the life of all creation and recognize its uniqueness. Knowing that it matters what we do, may I seek to engage in ethical activities and livelihoods that support the ecology of nature, balance and wholeness.

7. The Dharma of Tolerance

I hold the aspiration to train myself in Tolerance.

May my mind be open to recognize and value the journeys of others and actively cultivate patience and tolerance with all my relations. May I cultivate interactions of non-violence and come to know stillness when hearing the views of others. May this open mind blossom through direct experience, personal reflection and contemplation. On this path may I respect the choices of others and by neither action nor words shall I seek to hinder the path of another.

8. The Dharma of Obligation

I hold the aspiration of Sacred Obligation.

May I recognize the value in honoring obligations made, to carry these to completion and to have the integrity to communicate when circumstances change. I vow to take responsibility for all my actions and to carry these out to the best of my ability. In all my interactions may I have the motivation of personal integrity. By honoring my obligations, may this build strength of character and nurture the integral way.

9. The Dharma of Community

I hold the aspiration to Support the Community of Peace.

I honor the community of friends on the path. May I recognize the inherent value of community, the sustenance and support this brings and seek new ways of cultivating right relationships. May I be a spiritual friend to many and help to build bonds, which serve the community for peace.

10. The Dharma of the Senses
(The Body of Mindfulness)

I hold the aspiration to train myself in awareness of the senses.

May I recognize the value of nurturing and supporting my body and train myself to be ever aware of how substances affect my body, emotions and mind. May I use my senses to support life and use my vital energy to bring pleasure and joy respectfully to others.

Dedication of the Merit:
**Aided by these worthy aspirations may I be a
living example and generate the mind for peace.**

Dr. Usui's Reiki Principles

Dr. Usui adopted five admonitions to live by which were adapted from the Meiji Emperors precepts. Usui stated that if they were applied with Reiki, would heal the body, bring peace of mind, and happiness in life.

The following are those admonitions, taught as the Reiki Principles, Precepts or Ideals.

The following statement was written on Usui Sensei's memorial: "*When it comes to teaching, first let the student understand well the Meiji Emperor's admonitory, then in the morning and in the evening let them chant and have in mind the five admonitions which are:*

Don't get angry today.

Don't be grievous.

Express your thanks.

Be diligent in your business.

Be kind to others

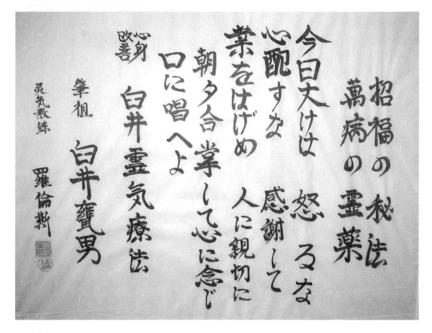

A western translation for the Kanji above is from an original document in Usui Sensei's handwriting and translates as follows:

The secret art of inviting happiness

The miraculous medicine of all diseases

Just for today, do not anger

Do not worry and be filled with gratitude

Devote yourself to your work. Be kind to people

Every morning and evening, join your hands in prayer

Pray these words to your heart and chant these words with your mouth

Usui Reiki Treatment for the improvement of body and mind.

Reiki Healing Clinics

The Reiki healing clinic is one of the many services offered by the Institute. Some of the ways the healing clinics benefit are as follows:

- A practice ground for Reiki students to hone their practical Reiki skills.
- A low cost service to the community from competent and qualified practitioners.
- The ongoing education and promotion of Reiki and its benefits to the community.
- The clinics give the general public an opportunity to experience Reiki, and to ask questions before they invest time and money into Reiki training.
- The clinics assist in generating positive energy and healing, as well as contributing to peace and healing throughout the community.
- Students can develop their abilities and are mentored by senior practitioners.

So far the Reiki Institute has participated in establishing several Reiki clinics in hospitals in urban & rural areas, for cancer patients, and for special interest groups in the spiritual and alternative arena.

The Future

The practice of Reiki has made tremendous movements in the West for over 30 years and has seen a great deal of change and expansion in a variety of forms. From the historical discoveries of Dr. Usui's teachings, to the new Reiki styles and healing systems that have emerged from the original teachings, Reiki continues to grow and to be a driving force to assist humanity in this modern and troubled age.

The essential factor in all of this is healing. In a modern world, with so many stresses on the environment and in personal and spiritual lives, Reiki in its essence remains a healing power of beauty, simplicity and unconditional love. Where it will take us is unknown; however, one thing is certain, and that is the ongoing exploration of Reiki. With our innate curiosity as human beings, we can only move a further step forward to understanding the great mystery of existence.

Want to Know More?

If you have enjoyed this book and would like to know more of the Institutes activities such as:

• Becoming an Associate Member of the IIRT
• Subscribing to our quarterly Reiki Newsletter
• Learning Reiki or upgrading your existing Reiki Certification
• Taking Reiki Master Teacher Training
• Learning Reiki Online
• Or would be interested in hosting IIRT Reiki Seminars in your country in the future, world-wide teaching tours occur bi-annually in the following areas: United States, Europe, United Kingdom, Asia, Australia and New Zealand.

For more details on any of these topics, please write to:

Address: The International Institute for Reiki Training, Directors Office, C/O PO Box 548 Fremantle Western Australia 6959.

Email: (Australia) reiki@ozzienet.net
or Email (International): reikihealerbook@hotmail.com

Web: visit our International Reiki Institute website online at: www.taoofreiki.com

TEMPLE AT MT. KURAMA

VIEW FROM MT. KURAMA

REIKI'S ROOTS. TREES ON THE PATH TO THE SUMMIT OF MT. KURAMA

A P P E N D I C E S

BIBLIOGRAPHY

Arai, Abbot Yusei, *Shingon Esoteric Buddhism, A Handbook for Followers*, Rt. Rev. Iwatsubo Shinko, Director, Department of Education of Koyasan Shingon Mission (Kongobuji), 1997

Austin, Jennie, *Practicing Reiki*, Geddes and Grosset, UK, 1999

Barnao, Vasudeva and Kadambii, *Australian Flower Essences for the 21st Century*, Australian Flower Essence Academy, Perth, Australia, 1997

Brennan, Barbara Ann, *Hands of Light, A Guide to Healing Through the Human Energy Field*, Bantam Book, 1988

Dhammapada, The, Element, 1997

Frederic, Louis, *Buddhism*, (Flammarion Iconographic Guides,) Flammarion, Paris-New York, 1995

Lama, Dalai, His Holiness the, *The Good Heart*, Rider Books, London, 1996

Locke, Ph.D., Dr. Ralph, *Personal Medicine*, SCI Publication, Chapel Hill, North Carolina, 2000

Lübeck, Walter, *Reiki, Way of the Heart*, Lotus Press, Shangri-La, 1996

McMahon, Tony, *Vessantara, Meeting the Buddhas, A Guide to Buddhas, Bodhisattvas and Tantric Deities*, Windhorse Publications, 1993

Millman, Dan, *Everyday Enlightenment*, Warner Books, 1999

Parkes, Chris and Penny, *Reiki: The Essential Guide to the Ancient Healing Art*, Vermillion, London, 1998

Petter, Frank Arjava, *Reiki Fire*, Lotus Press, Shangri-La, 1997

Petter, Frank Arjava, *Reiki, the Legacy of Dr. Usui*, Lotus Press, Shangri-La, 1998

Ponder, Catherine, *Healing Secrets of the Ages*, Second Edition, Devorss Publications, 1985

Quest, Penelope, *Reiki*, Piatkus, London, 1999

Rand, William Lee, *Reiki, The Healing Touch, First and Second Degree Manual*, Revised and Expanded Edition, Vision Publications, 2000

Rangdrol, Tsele Natsok, *The Mirror of Mindfulness, The Cycle of the Four Bardos*, Shambhala, Boston, 1989

Ray, Ph.D., Barbara, *The Reiki Factor,* Second Edition, Radiance Associates, St. Petersburg, Florida, 1986

Rinpoche, Kalu, *Luminous Mind, the Way of the Buddha*, Wisdom Publications, Boston, 1997

Rinpoche, Translated by Khenpo Konchog Gyaltsen, *The Jewel Ornament of Liberation, The Wish-Fulfilling Gem of the Noble Teachings*, Snow Lion Publications, Ithaca, New York, 1998

Rinpoche, Namgyal, *The Breath of Awakening, A Guide to Liberation through Anapanasati Mindfulness of Breathing*, Bodhi Publishing, Kinmount, Ontario, 1992

Rinpoche, Namgyal, *The Womb, Karma and Transcendence, A Journey Towards Liberation*, Bodhi Publishing, Kinmount, Ontario, 1996

Rinpoche, Sogyal, *The Tibetan Book of Living and Dying*, Rider Books, London, 1992

Rowland, Amy Z., *Traditional Reiki for Our Times*, Healing Arts Press, Rochester, Vermont, 1998

Stein, Diane, *Essential Reiki, A Complete Guide to an Ancient Healing Art*, The Crossing Press Inc., Freedom, CA, 1995

Sui, Choa Kok, *Pranic Healing*, Red Wheel/Weiser, York Beach, Maine, 1991

REFERENCE MANUALS

The Reiki Alliance Manual. Paul Mitchell 1985. Reiki Alliance.

Traditional Japanese Reiki as taught by David King and the TJR website: www.japanese-reiki.org

Franz and Bronwen Stiene. The International House of Reiki website: www.reiki.net.au

Translation of the Usui Memorial – Japanese Reiki Master Hyakuten Inamoto

Reiki III Reiki Master Course with Brian and Carole Daxter, 1993.

The Official Reiki Handbook, The official Reiki Program. A complete Reference Manual for students of Reiki. Barbara Ray, Ph.D., 1983.

Newlife Reiki Seichim and Newlife Seichim Manuals. Living Light Energy. Margot 'Deepa' Slater 1991.

Newlife Reiki Master Teacher Training with Margot 'Deepa' Salter, 1995.

A Japanese Reiki article published in Japan in 1986

'Iyashi No Te', by Toshitaka Mochizuki, 1995.

A Japanese article published in 1928, written by Shouoh Matsui, titled: 'A treatment to heal disease, hand healing'.

'History of Japanese Religion', by Masaharu Anesaki, 1963.

'Shingon, Japanese Esoteric Buddhism', by Taiko Yamasaki, 1988.

The life story of Mikao Usui, by Gejong Palmo, Master of Reiki. 1997, the Way of Reiki.

Medicine Buddha Sadhana, thanks and appreciation to: Ven. Zasep Tulku Rinpoche, Ven. Geshe Sonam Rinchen, Ven. Jampa Gendun.

GLOSSARY

Abbot: The principle or head teacher of a monastery in Buddhist traditions.

Amida Buddha: see Amitabha.

Amitabha Buddha: (Sanskrit) The Buddha of boundless light and boundless love. Among the five Buddha families, he belongs to the padma or lotus family and resides in the pure realm of Dewachen.

Aurora: (Sanskrit) The medicinal herb held in the right hand of Medicine Buddha, symbolizing healing. Also a common herb used in Indian Ayurvedic medicine.

Avalokiteshvara: (Sanskrit) The Buddha of compassion, love and kindness. Among the Bodhisattvas, Avalokiteshavara is perhaps the most venerated Buddhist deity.

Baihui: An acu-point found on the top of the head, the Baihui is the governing acupuncture point and is the location of the crown chakra.

Bardo: (Tibetan) The state between two other states of being. In particular the intermediate state between one life and the next.

Bodhisattva: (Sanskrit) A key religious concept of Mahayana Buddhism. A Bodhisattva, having developed compassion for all sentient beings, is a person who is on the way to perfecting their own Buddha nature. Thus, he or she has dedicated his or her life to the well-being of others, having vowed to lead all sentient beings to complete liberation. This term also describes particular Buddhist Deities who assist sentient beings from their suffering.

Bodhisattva Vow: The compassionate wish to forgo enlightenment until all beings are liberated from Samsara.

Buddha: Literally, 'the awakened one'. One who has attained Supreme Enlightenment; the embodiment of all virtues and perfection. Also the name of the historical Buddha, the spiritual teacher, Gautama Sakyamuni (563 B.C.)

Burdurya Probassa Buddha: (Sanskrit) Another name for Medicine Buddha. Literally, 'the Buddha of Lapis Lazuli Radiance'. See Medicine King Buddha.

Chakra: (Sanskrit) Wheel, center, eye, energy nexis within the subtle energy body.

Chenrezigi: (Tibetan) The Buddha of compassion. He is the patron and protector of Tibet and also a meditation deity, whose practice is very widespread, Tibetans believe that all successive Dalai Lamas are human manifestations of this deity.

Chi Kung: A Chinese style of energy work involving stances, visualization, breath work and slow Tai Chi - like movements to cultivate a balance of elemental energies in the body for health and long life.

Dalai Lama: Literally 'ocean of wisdom' is the title given to the supreme authority of Tibet. The lineage of the Dalai Lamas has continued without interruption up to the present fourteenth holder of this title: His Holiness Tenzin Gyatso, born in July 1935. The Dalai Lamas are emanations of Chenrezigi, the Buddha of compassion, who is the patron and protector of Tibet.

Dewachen: A pure land or realm of Buddha Amitabha and Chenrezigi. The practices and wishes with them direct the mind at the time of death to be reborn there, liberated from samsara.

Dharma: (Sanskrit) Derived from the etymological root meaning 'to hold', Dharma denotes the teachings of the Buddha, the 'truth' or the 'way', and the practice of those teachings. The Dharma holds us back from suffering and its causes. The Tibetan equivalent 'Chhos' literally means 'change' or 'transformation' and refers to both the process of spiritual transformation and the transformed result.

Geshe: (Tibetan) A term to describe a monk who has attained a high level of accomplishment in doctrinal learning and has had many years of monastic education. Its literal meaning is 'spiritual friend'.

Guru: (Sanskrit) A title to represent a spiritual teacher and mentor of high accomplishment, who has unshakable spiritual virtue and wisdom. The minimum qualities a guru must possess are compassion towards the student, inner discipline, a degree of serenity, and more knowledge on the subject that is being taught than is possessed by the student.

Hara: (Sanskrit) Refers to the energy center situated just below the navel. Also referred to as the Sacral Chakra, it is associated with the seat of personal power and vital life force.

Hinayana: (Sanskrit) Literally meaning 'lesser vehicle'. One of the three levels of Buddhism, its emphasis is on purification and individual liberation, which acts as a foundation for the other two levels, Mahayana and Vajrayana. The Hinayana Buddhist tradition is most prominent in the southern schools of Buddhism, namely Sri

Lanka, Thailand, Burma, Cambodia, Indonesia and Vietnam.

Kalpa: (Sanskrit) Generically, an aeon or other nearly limitless length of time. In Buddhist cosmology, it has the specific meaning of a complete cycle of a universe (a mahakalpa or 'great' kalpa consisting of four stages: emptiness, formation, maintenance, and destruction. Each of the four stages consists of twenty intermediate kalpas (antahkalpas), each of which increases and declines.)

Kanji: The Japanese word for Japanese pictographs or writings.

Karma: (Sanskrit) Karma refers to an important metaphysical concept related to action and its consequences. Literally meaning, 'action'. Whether these are physical, verbal or mental acts they imprint habitual tendencies in the mind. Upon meeting with suitable conditions, these habits ripen and manifest in the future.

Lama: (Tibetan) See Guru.

Mahayana: (Sanskrit) The 'great way' or 'great vehicle'. Those schools of Buddhism that teach the Bodhisattva ideal — of selfless striving to gain enlightenment so as to be in the best possible position to help all other living beings to be released from Samsara.

Manjushri: The Buddha of wisdom. His name means 'The Bodhisattva of Beautiful Splendor'. He is traditionally depicted wielding the sword of wisdom with his right arm while in the left he holds the stem of a lotus flower on which rests the Perfection of Wisdom Sutra.

Mantra: a string of sound-symbols recited to concentrate and protect the mind. Many Buddhist figures have mantras associated with them; through reciting their mantra one deepens one's connection with the aspect of Enlightenment which the figure embodies.

Medicine King Buddha: In Sanskrit his name means 'the Buddha of the Master of Medicine'. Medicine Buddha (Yakushi Nyorai, in Japan) is the Buddha who offers medicine to beings suffering from illness, and grants nourishment to the mind and body. As a Buddha who carries out the functions of a physician among a large number of Buddha's, he holds a medicine container in his left hand. In his right hand is held the Aurora herb with his hand held in the mudra of granting vows.

Meridians: A term to describe the energetic channels of the body.

Mudra: (Sanskrit) Describes movement, gesture, seal, stamp, impression. Usually refers to specific positions of the fingers or gestures, each signifying a particular aspect of dharma; also dance postures and positions of the whole body.

Nirvana: (Sanskrit) Literally: 'extinction', to cease, to blow, to extinguish. That dharma which remains after complete craving has been eradicated; the emancipation from all sorrows; extinction of all roots of unwholesomeness, namely, greed, hatred and delusion.

Pali: The language of Northern India in which the Buddha taught; subsequently used to transmit and preserve the teachings; later written, i.e. The Pali Canon.

Phowa: A High Tantric practice of Vajrayana Buddhism. The ejection of consciousness to a Buddha-field at the moment of death. Also referred to as 'Conscious Dying'.

Prajnaparamita: The 'Perfection of Wisdom', direct intuitive insight into the true nature of things, through which one overcomes ignorance and thereby the principle of suffering. In Tantric Buddhism it is also the name of a female deity who is the embodiment of the Perfection of Wisdom.

Refuge: Describes One's confidence in the precious ones, the three jewels: The Buddha, Dharma, and Sangha.

Sadhu: A traditional name for a holy man. Typically, in Hinduism, an ascetic who dedicates his life to spiritual self mortification, often performing daily spiritual practices of an extreme nature, in aid of purifying the body and mind.

Samsara: (Sanskrit) Literally: 'perpetual wandering'; the uncontrolled cycle of birth and death in which sentient beings driven by unwholesome actions and conflicting emotions repeatedly perpetuate their own suffering. Cyclic existence.

Sangha: (Sanskrit) The term Sangha refers to the community of practitioners of the Buddhist path. As one of the three Refuges, it refers to the Arya or Noble Sangha, those Buddhist practitioners who have gained insight into the true nature of things and whose progress towards Buddhahood is certain. In other contexts the term can refer to those who have taken ordination as Buddhist monks or nuns.

Sangle Mendela: See Medicine King Buddha.

Sanskrit: Describes the ancient Indic language that is the classical language of India.

Sensei: A term to describe a teacher of Traditional healing, Martial or Spiritual arts.

Shakyamuni Buddha: The 'sage of the Shakyans', an epithet of Gautama Siddhartha, the founder of Buddhism.

Shiatsu: A Japanese form of massage, as a complete system of healing through touch, drawing extensively on key aspects of traditional Chinese medicine. A nurturing massage promoting health by influencing the body's natural flow of energy via the energy pathways known as meridians.

Shingon: Established in Japan during the Heian period (AD 794-1185) by the spiritual master Kodo Dashi. The path of Shingon is to realize Buddhahood in this very life, to dedicate to the wellness and happiness of all beings and to establish the world of Buddha on earth. The word Shingon literally means: 'true words' and refers that the teachings are based on the words of the Buddha.

Shogun: (Japanese) One of a line of military governors ruling Japan until the revolution of AD 1867-68.

Sutra: (Sanskrit) (from the same root as sota, to hear). The written discourses of Buddha Shakyamuni, constituting all the teachings.

Tai Chi: Popular throughout Asia, Tai Chi consists of slow flowing movements that follow a set pattern. Often linked to martial arts.

Tantra: Literally: 'thread'; Vajrayana teachings outlining mystic practices as the most direct way to enlightenment. A form of Buddhism making use of yogic practices of visualization, mantra, mudra, and mandalas, as well as symbolic ritual, and meditations that work with subtle psychophysical energies. Also the Buddhist texts in which these practices are described.

Tendai: The name of the Sect which formed in Japan during the Heian period (AD 794-1185). Tendai was founded by Saicho (AD 767-822) Formal title: Dengyo Dashi. The path of Tendai is to attain Buddhahood through the practice of chanting sutra, meditation, precepts and esoteric Buddhism.

Transpersonal: Extending or going beyond the personal or individual. Also describes a movement of modern psychology derived from Jungian Psychology.

Tulku: (Tibetan) Literally: 'Emanation Body'. A tulku is a reincarnate Lama; that is, one who has been formally recognized as the reincarnation of his or her predecessor. A tulku has the ability to direct their next rebirth.

Vajrasattva: (Sanskrit) A Buddhist Tantric archetype of purification. Literally: 'Diamond Being'; a being of utter purity dwelling in the complete union of wisdom with the skill and means to awaken this in others.

Vajrayana: (Sanskrit) Literally: 'Diamond Vehicle'; the instantaneous, direct path of awakening and transcending all duality. One of the three levels of Buddhism, it is distinguished by its variety of practices to bring a being quickly to liberation.

Wonkur: (Tibetan) Empowerment Transmission. An initiation in which a specific enlightened mind-energy-body state is invoked by the Lama and transmitted to the student.

CONTACT DETAILS

If you would like to contact the author, Lawrence is more than happy to personally respond to any comments or questions on Reiki.

Please write to:

The International Institute for Reiki Training,
C/O PO Box 548 Fremantle Western Australia 6959.

Email (Australia): reiki@ozzienet.net or
Email (International): reikihealerbook@hotmail.com

Or

Visit our International Reiki Institute website
online at: www.taoofreiki.com

Reiki Meditations
for Beginners

by Lawrence Ellyard

Reiki Meditations for Beginners offers for the first time a practical guide to the practice of Meditation and Reiki. It provides the reader with the practical 'know how' and teaches the basics of meditation practice combined with an introduction to Reiki. The book is divided into three sections which include: An introduction to Reiki, an introduction to Meditation practice and section three includes a total of 25 Reiki Meditations.

Trade Paper   ISBN 978-0-9102-6197-5   152 pp pb $12.95

Available at bookstores and natural food stores nationwide or order your copy directly by sending $12.95 plus $2.50 shipping/handling ($.75 s/h for each additional copy ordered at the same time) to:

Lotus Press, PO Box 325, Dept. RH, Twin Lakes, WI 53181 USA
toll free order line: 800 824 6396 office phone: 262 889 8561
office fax: 262 889 2461 email: lotuspress@lotuspress.com
website: www.lotuspress.com

Lotus Press is the publisher of a wide range of books and software in the field of alternative health, including Ayurveda, Chinese medicine, herbology, aromatherapy, Reiki and energetic healing modalities. Request our free book catalog.